HVAC

FOR BEGINNERS 2024

From Warmth to Coolness: Navigating Heating, Ventilation, and Air Conditioning

Bryant A. Boughton

Copyright © 2023 Bryant A. Boughton- All rights reserved.

No part of this publication may be reproduced, stored in a retrieval system or transmitted in any form or by any means, electronic, mechanical, photocopying, recording, and scanning without permission in writing by the author

Contents

Introduction 1

Chapter 1 2

What Does HVAC Stand For? 2

    What Do HVAC Systems Do? 2

    Components of HVAC Systems 10

Chapter 2 13

Difference Between Conduction, Convection, and Radiation 13

    How Does Temperature Transfer In An HVAC System? 27

    Human Thermal Comfort 30

Chapter 3 39

Home Heating Fuel: Comparing Heating Oil, Gas, and Electric ... 39

    How Is Floor Heating That Is Powered Installed? 51

    How to Safeguard Yourself Against Common HVAC Scams ... 55

    What Is A Heat Pump 62

Chapter 4 72

The Importance Of Proper Ventilation In Commercial And Industrial Buildings 72

    Common Issues Associated With Poor Ventilation 78

    Main components of a ventilation system 82

The Basics Of Air Filtration In HVAC Design 84

What Airborne Contaminants Do HVAC Systems Remove? 87

Chapter 5 92

The Refrigeration Cycle 92

Types Of Air Conditioners 119

What Is A Ductless Air Conditioner? 142

Chapter 6 What are HVAC controls and how do they work? 157

Smart Thermostats 168

Different Types of Programmable Thermostats 173

How Zoning Can Improve Your HVAC Energy Efficiency 176

Chapter 7 180

Guide to HVAC Energy Efficiency 180

What Is HVAC Energy Efficiency? 180

Why Is HVAC Maintenance Important? 188

Chapter 8 195

Most Common HVAC Problems 195

HVAC Troubleshooting Guide: What to Do Before Calling a Pro 201

Chapter 9 206

Your Residential HVAC System; Types, Considerations, and Finding the Right Contractor 206

How Does a Commercial HVAC System Work?...................... 214

Types of HVAC Systems for Commercial Buildings 217

How Commercial HVAC Differs From Residential HVAC 222

Common Commercial HVAC Problems 226

Chapter 10 234

Advancements in HVAC System Technology........................... 234

Sustainable HVAC systems in commercial construction: balancing comfort and energy efficiency 242

Benefits Of Transforming Your Properties Into Smart Buildings 247

Introduction

Heating, ventilation, and air conditioning are known as HVAC. The three processes of heat addition, heat extraction, and conditioning are all integrated into the HVAC systems. Your home's temperature and humidity are controlled by its HVAC system. Buildings are much more comfortable to live in when they have HVAC systems.

This guide will talk about the basic ideas behind HVAC systems like heaters, air conditioners, and heat pumps, as well as the most important parts of these systems. Professionals should build and fix your HVAC system, but if you know how it works in general, you'll be better able to take care of it.

Chapter 1

What Does HVAC Stand For?

HVAC stands for air conditioning, ventilation, and heating. It's a catch-all word for any indoor air conditioning or heating system. HVAC systems enhance interior air quality and control humidity. Below is a definition of these terms:

- **Heating:** Potential parts of a home's heating system include radiators, space heaters, heat pumps, boilers, and furnaces.
- **Ventilation:** To distribute cleaned air throughout a facility, a number of HVAC units are connected to a ducting system. A ventilation system also includes chimneys and vents.
- **Air conditioning:** In addition to central air conditioning units, ductless mini-split air conditioning systems, window units, and wall units can also be used to reduce interior temperature.

What Do HVAC Systems Do?

Your home most likely has some sort of HVAC system unless you reside somewhere with year-round mild temps and ideal natural ventilation. The maintenance of a comfortable indoor temperature is the most evident role of an HVAC system. In areas with extreme weather conditions, this may potentially become a health and safety concern. These systems can remove or add moisture, filter out particles and waste, and heat or chill the air.

How Function HVAC Systems?

The operation of a few popular HVAC system types is shown here.

The air conditioner

Refrigerant is used by air conditioners to remove heat from homes. When the refrigerant passes through the air handler, which is the inside section of an air conditioning machine, it is a liquid. Up until the refrigerant transforms into a gas, heat is extracted from the air in the air handler. After that, the heat is discharged into the outside air by a condenser, an outside device. The refrigerant is subsequently transformed back into a liquid by the compressor, allowing it to move indoors and carry out the cycle once more.

Heating Furnace

Fuel is burned in furnaces to produce heat. The most widely used fuels are heating oil, natural gas, and liquid propane. While some might function solely on electricity, almost all of them need some electrical input to operate the controls. The majority of furnaces are forced-air units, meaning that a blower circulates warm air through the air ducts in the house. By capturing dust and particles, a filter maintains the furnace's efficiency and cleans the air.

Heat Pump

Similar to an air conditioner, a heat pump transfers heat and maintains a home's temperature by using refrigerant. Heat pumps, as opposed to air conditioning systems, have the ability to warm a house during the winter by drawing heat from the ground or, in the case of a geothermal heat pump, the outside air. They don't need exhaust vents or pilot lights because they don't burn fuel like a furnace does. A heat pump and furnace can be used together in colder climates to provide heat on particularly chilly days.

HVAC System Types

Although there are numerous varieties of heating and air conditioning systems, residential structures typically have these. If an HVAC system is ducted, treated air must be distributed throughout the building via a ducting system. Alternatively, it might transmit treated air ductlessly, eliminating the need for these unique conduits.

Heater

Similar in operation to furnaces, boilers heat water by burning fuel rather than air. The water in the boiler, which is then heated by electricity, gas, or oil, is pumped through the radiators in your house to heat every room. In certain boiler systems, steam is circulated rather than water. The water or steam is returned to the boiler to be heated again after cooling.

In order to maximize energy efficiency, boilers can be coupled with a home's water heater to create more heat while using less fuel than furnaces. Boiler systems need different maintenance and safety inspections than conventional HVAC systems, and they are more expensive to install and repair. Although the majority of contemporary boilers have significant safety features, they can still be potentially deadly in the event of a malfunction. Boilers generate a lot of heat and pressure.

Central air conditioning unit

Cooled air can circulate throughout a building thanks to central air conditioning units that are connected to a duct system. There is a thermostat in charge of them: The device will activate and chill the air until the temperature decreases once again if it gets above a predetermined point.

By chilling the air, air conditioners remove humidity from it. The moisture in the air turns into condensation that accumulates on the evaporator coils as the refrigerant moves through the components of the indoor system. This condensation eventually turns into water droplets, which land in a drip pan and exit through an outside drain.

In warmer areas, central air conditioning systems are quite useful for controlling indoor temperatures. Air filters in the system filter out dust, pollen, and other possible allergens when air is forced through them. Sadly, installing central air conditioning systems and the ductwork that goes with them is costly, and operating them consumes a lot of energy. Additionally, air ducts need to be cleaned professionally once in a while to prevent the growth of mold, mildew, and vermin.

Ductless Mini-Split System

Ductless mini-split air conditioning systems are designed to cool one or more rooms. They need one or more inside air handlers and an outdoor condenser unit, just like central air conditioning. But having no ductwork also means cleaning less and not having to drill holes in the walls, ceilings, or floors to install air ducts. The majority of mini-splits are cheap and simple to place on the wall, however this means they occupy wall space and are readily noticeable.

Though they are less effective and consume less energy than central air conditioning units, mini-splits are less practical in warm areas. If you only want to chill one or a few rooms in your house, live in a milder climate, and your property lacks ductwork, a mini-split air conditioner is typically the best option.

Electric Heat Pump

Heat pumps, despite their name, are used for both heating and cooling. They require roughly 50% less electricity to provide the same amount of heat as a furnace or baseboard heater, according to the U.S. Department of Energy. Although ductless heat pumps that resemble mini-splits in appearance and operation have been made possible by recent technological advancements, they can still deliver central heating through the existing ductwork.

You can reduce your energy costs by using a heat pump, but they are most effective in areas that don't frequently endure below-freezing temperatures. Because they don't burn fossil fuels, there is no carbon monoxide risk, and they are a greener option than furnaces. Nevertheless, the cost of installation is high.

A window air conditioner

The condenser and air handler are combined into one unit in a window air conditioning system, making it an all-in-one setup. As it cools the air inside the room, the unit sits in the window and vents hot air outdoors. Although they can only cool one room at a time, these air conditioners are more efficient than others. They are simple to locate and install and require little upkeep.

Additionally, they occupy window space, and not everyone finds a big piece of machinery in the window attractive. Concerning higher floors is the possibility of the unit falling out and causing damage. Because of the partially opened window, they can pose a security risk on bottom floors. On the other hand, if you have a tight budget and need to chill a tiny room, a window unit is typically the least priced alternative.

Heating and Cooling Packages

Certain central HVAC systems consist of a single unit, usually located outside, that houses both the heating and cooling components. It could be an air conditioner with extra heat strips on the interior air handler to supply warm air as needed, or it could be a heat pump with additional evaporator coils to provide additional cooling.

Compared to split systems, which have indoor and outdoor units, packaged systems are less frequent. Because they take up less room and are typically less expensive to install than split systems, they are most frequently utilized in compact homes. Additionally, they are usually less efficient, and because every part is outside, the environment and weather can wear them down more.

Components of HVAC Systems

Certain components of many HVAC system types remain the same. The most crucial parts of the system and their purposes are listed below.

- **Thermostat:** By automatically determining when to start and stop your HVAC system, the thermostat on your system enables you to change the temperature in your house. Thermostats, which can be either digital or analog, are a common control system used in almost all HVAC systems. With a smart thermostat, you can control the temperature of your house from anywhere in the globe.
- **Air exchanger:** By enabling fresh air to enter your home's HVAC system, this part enhances ventilation. It extracts humidity from the ducting to assist stop the growth of mold and mildew. Stale air is also vented outside.
- **Refrigerant:** This material is used by heat pumps and air conditioners to transmit heat both inside and outside. A heat exchanger is used by the HVAC system's machinery to shift refrigerant from a liquid to a gas and back again in order to transfer heat.

- **Evaporator coils:** To extract heat and moisture from the air, liquid refrigerant passes through the indoor evaporator coils of an air conditioner. The refrigerant turns into a gas when it warms up.
- **Condenser:** The external condenser unit of the air conditioner receives the gaseous refrigerant after that. The compressor forces the refrigerant back into a liquid state inside the condenser. After then, it can go back inside to absorb more heat.
- **Blower:** To move air through the ducts or the living area of your house, forced-air furnaces and air conditioners both need a blower motor and fan.

DIY vs. Professional HVAC Installation

HVAC installation is typically a task best left to the pros. This is the reason.

Expert Installation of HVAC Systems

To install and maintain HVAC systems, HVAC technicians require a valid license. It's a difficult procedure that calls for specific skills and equipment. Installing ducting for central heating and cooling systems usually necessitates making structural incisions into the house. To guarantee a ductless system operates effectively, all components must be correctly anchored, linked, and tested. Because

HVAC systems use a lot of energy to operate, trying to install one on your own could result in expensive energy bills or a malfunctioning system.

Do It Yourself HVAC Setup

Installing a window AC unit is one HVAC task that most homeowners can complete. The majority of these devices are offered for sale as kits that include all necessary components and window anchoring instructions. You can engage an HVAC specialist to conduct the installation if the unit is too heavy or if you prefer a more inconspicuous, long-lasting installation.

Our Final Thought

For optimal temperature, mechanical ventilation, and airflow, the majority of residential and commercial structures are equipped with HVAC systems. A/C technicians are required to install, service, and clean common HVAC system components such as air conditioners, furnaces, heat pumps, boilers, and ducting. Get estimates from at least three local providers before selecting a reliable HVAC business.

Chapter 2

Difference Between Conduction, Convection, and Radiation

Have you ever seen the static electric phenomenon or the seaside breeze in the winter? Have you ever wondered how energy from the sun makes it to us after traversing such vast stretches of space? You've come to the perfect location if you've ever wondered about these things!

Conduction, convection, and radiation—the three fundamental ideas of heat transfer—are responsible for all of the aforementioned events.

The Greek philosopher made the first recorded observation of conduction in the sixth century BCE. We now know that the reason amber attracts lightweight items like feathers when it is rubbed with a cloth is because conduction transfers electrical charge. But scientists didn't start researching heat conduction until the 17th century.

Observations of natural phenomena like weather patterns, ocean currents, and the behavior of combustible materials led to the discovery of convection.

Finally, the 20th century saw the discovery of radiation considerably later. The French physicist Antoine Becquerel is credited with the discovery of radiation. He found that uranium potassium sulfate, a radiation mineral, released radiation in 1896 that could pass through things like paper and expose photographic plates. This discovery was made while the mineral was being studied for its qualities.

These discoveries have now greatly impacted our daily lives. All forms of technology employ these ideas in one way or another to simplify our lives.

Radiation, Convection, and Conduction

Heat is transferred through a substance by conduction, which occurs while the substance is not moving. For instance, conduction allows heat to be transported from a hot cooking vessel to your hand.

Convection is the movement-induced transmission of heat across a fluid, such as water or air. When an air conditioner is turned on, for instance, the heated air in the room is replaced with cooler air, which rises and creates a convection current that disperses heat throughout the space.

The Tabular Form of Conduction, Convection, and Radiation Differences

Parameters of Comparison	Conduction	Convection	Radiation
Mode of heat transfer	Heat transfer through direct contact with particles. The material of heat transfer is generally in a solid state.	involves the transfer of heat energy by the movement of a fluid or gas	Radiation involves the transfer of heat energy through electromagnetic waves.
Material properties	A material is a good conductor of heat if it has high thermal conductivity.	The convection coefficient determines the convective property of the fluid.	Properties like emissivity, radioactivity, absorption, and transmissivity determine a radioactive material.
Rate of heat transfer	Fast mode of heat transfer after convection.	Fastest mode of heat transfer.	Relatively slow mode of heat transfer.
The direction of heat flow	Heat is transferred from high-temperature to low-temperature material.	Heat is transferred from high-temperature to low-temperature material.	Heat is radiated in all directions.
Medium for heat transfer	Particle contact. Solid medium.	Fluids movement.	No medium is required. Can travel through a vacuum space.

Describe Conduction.

Heat is transported from one object to another via direct contact and is known as conduction, one of the three modes of heat transfer. Since the particles in solids like metals and ceramics are closely packed and easily transfer heat through direct contact, conduction is the primary mechanism of heat transmission in these materials. Heat is transported through a material medium during conduction from a location of higher temperature to a region of lower temperature. It is determined by the material's heat conductivity.

Heat causes a material's molecules to gain energy and vibrate more quickly, which leads to conduction. These molecules impart some of their energy to nearby molecules when they meet, which speeds up their own vibrations. Energy is transferred in this manner until the material as a whole reaches thermal equilibrium, which is characterized by constant temperature.

Many forms of conduction

Conduction falls into two categories:

1. The most prevalent kind of conduction, known as "conductive conduction," is the exchange of heat energy between two things that are in close

proximity to one another. Conduction of this kind happens in gases, liquids, and solids.

2. Convective conduction is the process by which heat energy is transferred from two objects separated by a fluid or gas. The gas or fluid acts as a medium via which heat energy is transferred. Both gases and liquid can conduct convective conduction.

3. Electron Conduction: Free electrons in some materials, like metals, travel around to transfer heat energy. Similar to how electricity travels along a wire, these unbound electrons can transfer thermal energy between different parts of the substance.

Thermal Conductivity

You must be aware that different materials have varying capacities for storing heat. Heat transfer has established the characteristic of specific heat C_p as a gauge for a material's thermal energy storage capacity. Similarly, a material's capacity to conduct heat is indicated by its thermal conductivity, or k. The rate of heat transmission through a unit thickness of the material per unit area per unit temperature difference is hence the definition of a material's thermal conductivity. A material's capacity to conduct heat is determined by its thermal conductivity. When a material's thermal conductivity is high, it means that it is an excellent heat conductor; when it is low, it means that it is an insulator or poor heat conductor.

Both excellent and poor conductors

Materials that facilitate easy heat transfer from one area of the material to another are considered good conductors of heat. The heat conductivity of these materials is high.

The great mobility of electrons in metals, such copper, aluminum, silver, and gold, enables heat to be transported through the substance quickly, making these materials good heat conductors. A few other materials that are effective heat conductors are diamond, graphite, and some ceramics.

Conversely, materials that are poor conductors—also referred to as insulators—make it difficult for heat to move through them. Because of their low thermal conductivity, insulators are frequently utilized to slow down the flow of heat. The following materials are examples of insulators: rubber, wood, plastic, and glass.

Heat transfer via these materials is impeded by their densely packed molecular structure.

How to Apply Good Conductors:

Electrical wire: Because they facilitate the efficient flow of electricity, excellent conductors like copper and aluminum are frequently utilized in power transmission and electrical wiring.

Cooking: To provide even heat distribution throughout the surface, cookware is made of good conductors like copper and aluminum.

Industrial operations: Because metals are good conductors and can withstand high temperatures and swiftly transfer heat, they are employed in a variety of industrial processes, including forging, smelting, and welding.

Heat exchangers: In heat-exchanging appliances such as air conditioners, freezers, boilers, heaters, and many other thermodynamic equipment, good conductors are essential.

Electronic devices: To make electrical connections and move heat away from delicate components, excellent conductors like copper and gold are employed in electronic devices.

Using Poor Conductors:

Insulation: To lessen heat transfer and increase energy efficiency, bad conductors like air, plastic, and rubber are employed as insulation in appliances and buildings.

Protective gear: To insulate against electric shock and heat, bad conductors like rubber and plastic are utilized in protective gear like gloves and boots.

Food storage: To keep food hot or cold by limiting heat transfer, food containers made of bad conductors like foam and plastic are utilized.

Overall, a variety of uses, including electrical wiring, insulation, and cooking, can benefit from the characteristics of good and bad conductors.

Describe Convection.

Energy transfer between a solid surface and a nearby moving liquid or gas is referred to as convection. It happens when the fluid's velocity and conduction—heat transmission through direct contact—combine. The quantity of heat transmitted by convection is directly influenced by the fluid's velocity of motion. Convection and conduction function similarly, but the medium used for heat transfer is where they differ most.

Heat transfer between the solid surface and the fluid is enhanced by bulk motion in the fluid. But it also makes figuring out the heat transfer rate more difficult.

Natural convection and forced convection are the two primary forms of convection.

Natural convection: This kind of convection happens when a fluid, like water or air, becomes heated from below, expanding and losing density. A natural circulation pattern is produced when the warmer, lighter fluid rises and the cooler, denser fluid falls. This mechanism generates wind and air currents by causing heated air to rise and cool air to sink.

Forced convection: This kind of convection happens when a fan, pump, compressor, or other external source pushes a fluid in a certain direction. In heating, ventilation, and air conditioning (HVAC) systems, heat or cold is distributed throughout a structure by means of circulating air or water through a fan or pump.

The fluid's flow, which transfers heat from the heat source to colder regions, improves heat transfer in both forced and natural convection. Numerous commercial and natural activities, such as food preparation, electronics cooling, and atmospheric temperature regulation, depend on this process.

There are many real-world uses for forced and natural convection in our daily lives, including manufacturing processes, food preparation, building heating and cooling, and more. Here are a few instances of how they are used:

Natural Convection's Applications

Atmospheric circulation: Wind and weather patterns are produced by the natural convection that moves the atmosphere of the Earth.

Cooking: To properly transfer heat and cook food, ovens and stoves employ natural convection.

Solar energy: Heat is transferred from the sun to a storage tank by natural convection, which is a mechanism employed in solar collectors to move water or air.

Ventilation: To control indoor air quality and provide ventilation, buildings use natural convection.

Forced Convection's Applications

HVAC systems: Heating, ventilation, and air conditioning (HVAC) systems employ forced convection to move water or air around and control humidity and temperature.

Electronics cooling: To keep computer processors and power amplifiers from overheating and to increase their longevity, forced convection is utilized to cool the components.

Industrial operations: To transport heat and regulate temperature, forced convection is employed in a variety of industrial processes, including food preparation, chemical processing, and metalworking.

Car engines: In order to circulate coolant and avoid overheating, forced convection is employed in car engines.

Heat transmission in forced and natural convection is facilitated by fluid movement, which can be attributed to external forces or buoyancy. Convection is hence a crucial process for controlling energy transfer and temperature in a range of environments.

Radiation: What Is It?

Radiation is the final method of heat transmission. The process by which energy is transferred through space or a medium as electromagnetic waves or particles is known as radiation. The primary distinction between radiation and other heat-transfer methods is that radiation transmits heat from one body to another without the use of a medium. Moreover, temperature potential is not necessary for heat transfer. Radiation can come in a variety of forms, such as radio waves, gamma rays, X-rays, and visible light. Depending on their body's composition and temperature, all bodies emit electromagnetic radiation, which can include microwaves, radio waves, infrared radiation, and visible light. The random motion of atoms and molecules within the body is the cause of this phenomena, which is referred to as thermal radiation. The temperature of the body affects both the amount and wavelength of radiation released; hotter bodies release more energy at shorter wavelengths.

There are several applications for radiation in different fields, such as:

1. Medical diagnosis and treatment: To see inside the body and identify medical disorders, medical

imaging methods such as X-rays, CT scans, and PET scans frequently involve radiation. Radiation therapy can also be used to treat cancer.
2. Nuclear power plants generate energy through regulated nuclear processes that result in heat, which is subsequently converted into electrical power. There is a utilization of radioactive radiation in this process.
3. Food preservation: By eliminating bacteria and other microbes that can contaminate food or spread illness, radiation can be used to preserve food. We call this procedure "food irradiation."
4. Industrial uses: Radiation is employed in a number of industrial processes, including the sterilisation of medical supplies and equipment, pipeline leak detection, and material quality control testing to check for flaws.
5. Scientific research: A wide range of applications of radiation are found in science, including the age determination of archaeological artifacts, the analysis of biological and chemical samples, and the study of matter's properties.
6. Space exploration: Radiation technology is employed in space communication for a number of

functions, including imaging, navigation, and communication.

Key Distinctions (In Points) Between Conduction, Convection, and Radiation

- When temperature differentials cause atoms in a medium to vibrate, conduction heat transfer takes place. When a temperature gradient is introduced to medium molecules, convection results from the molecules' natural mobility. On the other hand, radiation happens when a body produces heat and radiates it in all directions.
- While radiation can occur in a vacuum media, conduction and convection require a medium in order to transport heat.
- Radiation can be harmful if employed carelessly, but conduction and convection are generally safer forms of heat transfer.

In summary

Numerous applications in our daily lives are governed by the three mechanisms of heat transfer already stated. It might be the energy produced in nuclear power plants or the cooling effect of fans on perspiration during the heat. Although these concepts have been used by man for a very long time, we are now using them more effectively and developing technology.

How Does Temperature Transfer In An HVAC System?

The central HVAC system of today is incredibly effective. Many of the same parts are used in all of the operations, including the air conditioning, ventilation, and heating. This is due to the fact that HVAC equipment does more than just produce and pump air conditioning or heat into thin air (forgive the pun). Instead, it modifies the temperature by the passage of thermal energy, which is facilitated by a device known as a heat exchanger.

How Do Heat Exchangers Operate?

Despite its name, the heat exchanger plays a crucial role in both heating and cooling. Heat naturally transfers from warm to cold places, and your home's heat exchanger reverses this movement to allow your home to be either heated or cooled. Through the system's coils, thermal energy is transferred from one medium to another to operate. Heat exchangers work by heating the air with combustion gasses or cooling it with a cold fluid.

Conduction is the method used by an HVAC system's heat exchanger to transfer heat. This is the transfer of thermal energy via direct contact with a temperature source from one molecule to another. HVAC heat exchangers use conduction to either heat or cool the air, but they require the right medium to provide the energy. This typically takes the form of a refrigerant for cooling.

Cooling

Temperature transfers are how air conditioners transfer heat from indoor to outdoor environments. Warm air from an interior area is circulated by a fan over refrigerant-filled evaporator coils, causing the refrigerant to evaporate. when a result, the refrigerant absorbs heat from the air and releases it when it turns from a gas to a liquid, which is then dispersed throughout the house.

After that, the outside compressor and condenser get this chilly refrigerant. It becomes a heated gas in the compressor. Heat is removed from the condenser by air flowing over it as the gas enters the coils. Restarting the process, the refrigerant cycles again into a cool liquid.

Heating

It goes without saying that the temperature transfer for heating your system must operate in the opposite direction from that for air conditioning. Using an evaporator fan, it draws cool air through the heat exchanger, which is heated by gas or electricity. As it crosses the heat source, the cold air from your house absorbs heat and is re-distributed throughout the house.

The heat exchanger has an extra role during heating. It keeps gases isolated from the heated air if they are utilized in the combustion process. In order to keep your family safe, they must be freed by an exterior escape.

Human Thermal Comfort

Only when the people living in the buildings are comfortable will energy-efficient structures be considered effective. They will use alternatives to conventional heating, ventilation, and air conditioning (HVAC) systems, such as window-mounted air conditioners or space heaters, if they are uncomfortable. These alternatives may be far worse.

Because thermal comfort is so individualized, it is challenging to quantify. Variations in air temperature, humidity, radiant temperature, air velocity, metabolic rates, and garment levels all affect these perceptions, and each person's experience varies slightly depending on their physiology and state.

Thermal comfort, also known as human comfort, is the occupants' satisfaction with the surrounding thermal conditions and is crucial to take into account when designing a structure that will be occupied by people. It is defined as "that condition of mind which expresses satisfaction with the thermal environment and is assessed by subjective evaluation1" in the ANSI/ASHRAE Standard 55-2010.

When the body is hot, feeling chilly will be nice; but, if the body is already cold in the core, it will be unpleasant. In addition, not every part of the body has the same temperature of skin. Variations in blood flow and subcutaneous fat are reflected in differences in various body sections. The distribution and level of skin temperature are also significantly impacted by the insulating properties of clothes. As a result, feeling from any specific area of the skin will vary depending on the temperature of the environment, the time of day, the clothing worn, and the location.

Elements of Human Comfort

When planning for thermal comfort, there are six things to keep in mind. Among its deciding elements are the following:

- Metabolic rate (met): The body's energy production
- Clothes insulation (clo): The degree of thermal protection that an individual is donning
- Air temperature: The ambient temperature of the person in question

- Radiant temperature: The total temperature from all surfaces surrounding an occupant, weighted averaged
- Air velocity: The rate at which air moves across time and distance.
- Relative humidity: Airborne water vapor percentage

Temperature, radiant temperature, relative humidity, and air velocity are examples of environmental parameters. Clothes and metabolic rate (activity level) are personal considerations.

An energy balance for heat transport is used to calculate thermal comfort. Convection, conduction, and radiation heat transfer are all weighed against the occupant's metabolic rate. The human body has an area of 19 feet squared, or 1.81 square meters, where heat transfer takes place between the environment. The thermal perception is either "warm" or "hot" depending on whether more heat is entering or exiting the body. If more heat is leaving the body, the thermal perception is defined as "cold."

Ole Fanger created a technique known as Predicted Mean Vote (PMV) and Predicted Percentage of Dissatisfied (PPD) that describes thermal comfort.

Estimated Mean Voting

The term Predicted Mean Vote (PMV) refers to a temperature scale that was created by Fanger and subsequently approved as an ISO standard. It goes from Cold (-3) to Hot (+3). In order to get the initial data, a huge number of people—reportedly thousands of Israeli soldiers—were exposed to various circumstances within a climate chamber. They were then asked to choose a position on a scale that best reflected how comfortable they felt. The data were then used to create a mathematical model that represented the relationship between all of the physiological and environmental parameters taken into consideration. The following sensation scale is produced as a result of applying heat balance concepts to relate the size thermal comfort parameters to one another.

Value	Sensation
-3	Cold
-2	Cool
-1	Slightly cool
0	Neutral
1	Slightly warm
2	Warm
3	Hot

Predicted Mean Vote sensation scale

For an interior space, ASHRAE 55 recommends an acceptable PMV range of -0.5 to +0.5 for thermal comfort.

Expected Ratio of Unsatisfied

The percentage of occupants who will be unhappy with the thermal conditions is predicted by the Predicted Percentage of Dissatisfied (PPD). It is dependent on PMV since PPD rises when PMV deviates from 0, or neutral.

Since you can never please everyone all the time, the recommended acceptable PPD range for thermal comfort from ASHRAE 55 is less than 10% persons dissatisfied for an interior area. The maximum number of people unhappy with their comfort circumstances is 100%.

The Arithmetic of PPD and PMV

Perhaps the most popular thermal comfort index available today is PMV. In "Moderate Thermal Environments - Determination of the PMV and PPD Indices and Specification of the Conditions for Thermal Comfort," ISO Standard 7730 (ISO 1984) explicitly defines the comfort zone in terms of PMV limitations.

Only people who are exposed to constant conditions over an extended length of time with a steady metabolic rate can use the PMV equation.

PMV is computed using Fanger's thermal comfort model in the following formula.

$$PMV = [0.303e^{-0.036M} + 0.028]\{(M-W) - 3.96E^{-8}f_{cl}[(t_{cl}+273)^4 - (t_r+273)^4]$$
$$- f_{cl}h_c(t_{cl}-t_a) - 3.05[5.73 - 0.007(M-W) - p_a] - 0.42[(M-W)$$
$$- 58.15] - 0.0173M(5.87 - p_a) - 0.0014M(34 - t_a)\}$$

With

$$f_{cl} = \begin{matrix} 1.0 + 0.2I_{cl} \\ 1.05 + 0.1I_{cl} \end{matrix}$$

$$t_{cl} = 35.7 - 0.0275(M-W) - R_{cl}\{(M-W) - 3.05[5.73 - 0.007(M-W) - p_a]$$
$$- 0.42[(M-W) - 58.15] - 0.0173M(5.87 - p_a) - 0.0014M(34 - t_a)\}$$

$$R_{cl} = 0.155I_{cl}$$

$$h_c = 12.1(V)^{1/2}$$

When

e	Euler's number (2.718)
f_{cl}	clothing factor
h_c	convective heat transfer coefficient
I_{cl}	clothing insulation [clo]
M	metabolic rate [W/m²] 115 for all scenarios
p_a	vapor pressure of air [kPa]
R_{cl}	clothing thermal insulation
t_a	air temperature [°C]
t_{cl}	surface temperature of clothing [°C]
t_r	mean radiant temperature [°C]
V	air velocity [m/s]
W	external work (assumed = 0)

Given that PPD depends on PMV, it may be described as

$$PPD = 100 - 95e^{[-(0.3353 PMV^4 + 0.2179 PMV^2)]}$$

Adaptive Comfort

Adaptive comfort models incorporate more human behavior. They believe that people will typically adjust their behavior and take actions to make themselves more comfortable if changes in the thermal environment cause discomfort. These might be removing clothing, becoming less active, or even just opening a window. These models primarily broaden the scope of situations that architects can deem acceptable, particularly in naturally ventilated buildings where inhabitants enjoy more control over their indoor climate.

The space must have movable windows, no mechanical air conditioning, be nearly sedentary, and have individuals with met metabolic rates of 1.0 to 1.3 in order to qualify as adaptively comfortable. Additionally, residents can adjust their wardrobe to suit the temperature by adding or deleting items.

BEHAVIOR	EFFECT	OFFSET
Jumper/Jacket on or off	Changes Clo by ± 0.35	± 2.2K
Tight fit/Loose fit clothing	Changes Clo by ± 0.26	± 1.7K
Collar and tie on or off	Changes Clo by ± 0.13	± 0.8K
Office chair type	Changes Clo by ± 0.05	± 0.3K
Seated or walking around	Varies Met by ± 0.4	± 3.4K
Stress level	Varies Met by ± 0.3	± 2.6K
Vigour of activity	Varies Met by ± 0.1	± 0.9K
Different postures	Varies Met by ± 10%	± 0.9K
Consume cold drink	Varies Met by -0.12	+ 0.9K
Consume hot drink/food	Varies Met by +0.12	- 0.9K
Operate desk fan	Varies Vel by +2.0m/s	+ 2.8K
Operate ceiling fan	Varies Vel by +1.0m/s	+ 2.2K
Open window	Varies Vel by +0.5m/s	+ 1.1K

Table 1 - The effect of adaptive behaviors on optimum comfort temperatures. Taken from BRE

Chapter 3

Home Heating Fuel: Comparing Heating Oil, Gas, and Electric

It is imperative to undertake extensive study before choosing the best fuel to heat your home. To help you make an informed choice, we explore the distinctions between gas, electricity, and heating oil in this book. Let's start by giving a general introduction to heating oil.

An Overview of Gas, Electric, and Oil Heating

Because of its special qualities, residents in the Northeast continue to favor heating oil. It is said to burn cleanly and burns hotter than natural gas. Furthermore, heating oil furnaces are typically less expensive to run than electric furnaces.

Knowing About Heating Oil

Mid-range petroleum products include heating oil, which is derived from crude oil. It is comparable to diesel fuel in terms of composition and boiling range. Following the refining process, heating oil is delivered to nearby heating oil firms by pipelines, tank trucks, or railroad tank cars that are used to transfer it to oil terminals and storage facilities. In the United States, heating oil accounted for about 5.3 million households' principal fuel during the 2020–2021 timeframe.

The Benefits of Heating Oil

The efficiency of the fuel and the robustness of the heating systems themselves are responsible for the extended lifespan of oil heat systems. The following are the main benefits of utilizing an oil heat system:

Quick Heating: Heating oil heats homes more quickly than natural gas because it produces greater temperatures.

Greater Heat Output: When compared to some other fuels, heating oil generates more heat per gallon.

Accessibility in Remote Areas: Getting heating oil is simpler for those living in isolated areas.

Longevity & Cost Savings: Compared to gas units, heating oil systems usually have a longer lifespan and cost less money.

Safety and Clean Burning: Heating oil does not form soot indoors and is safe to use because it vaporizes at 140 degrees.

Drawbacks to Heating Oil

But every heating system has its shortcomings. The following are a few drawbacks of heating oil furnace use:

Fuel costs are subject to variations, as the value of refined crude oil on the global market affects the price of heating oil.

Cleaning Requirements: Heating oil systems require cleaning on a regular basis.

Oil Heat vs. Natural Gas Heat

Another common fossil fuel for heating is natural gas, which can be found in certain crude oil reservoirs, coal deposits, and rock formations. After extraction, it passes through processing at a plant and is then piped to suppliers all around the nation.

Natural Gas Heating's Benefits

When compared to alternative solutions, natural gas heating is more affordable and convenient. The following are some advantages of this kind of heating system:

Convenience: It is easy to get and use natural gas.

Savings: Generally speaking, natural gas is less expensive than electric heating.

The Drawbacks of Heating with Natural Gas

Natural gas heating is popular, however it has many disadvantages as well:

Increased Installation Costs: The costs associated with installing a gas connection are one reason why installing a natural gas furnace might be costly.

Impact on the environment: When a natural gas furnace runs, carbon dioxide is released.

Restricted Lifespan: In comparison to heating oil systems, natural gas furnaces typically have a 10 to 15 year lifespan.

The Distinctions Between Gas and Oil

The decision between natural gas and heating oil is influenced by a number of variables, such as cost and local availability. The main variations are as follows:

Cost Comparison: When comparing fuel pricing and heat output, heating oil is frequently less expensive than natural gas in many places.

Safety and Storage: Since heating oil vaporizes at 140 degrees and doesn't emit carbon monoxide, it's safer to use and store than natural gas.

Efficiency Gains: Over the previous three decades, household consumption has decreased by 33.6% because to advancements in heating oil systems.

Oil and Gas Furnaces: A Comparison

The cost of a natural gas furnace is often higher than that of a heating oil system. The cost of switching from oil to gas heating is another factor. Furthermore, natural gas furnaces may only last 10 to 15 years, whereas heating oil furnaces often have an average lifespan of 30 years or more.

Comparing Costs

When compared to natural gas, heating oil has historically been a competitive option. But it's crucial to remember that a gallon of heating oil produces 40% more BTUs of heat than the same volume of natural gas, so a fair comparison is required. When it comes to price for residential heating requirements, oil heating frequently ends up being the more economical choice.

Electric Heat versus. Heating Oil

In areas of the country with warmer winters—especially in the south—electric heating is typically preferred. Still, it's not a common option in the Northeast. This is a comparison between heating oil systems and electric heating:

The Benefits of Electric Heat

Certain advantages come with electric heat, mostly because it's so widely available:

Simple Operation and Maintenance: Electric furnaces need less maintenance.

Accessibility: Since most homes already have electricity, installing an electric furnace won't cost as much.

The drawbacks of using electric heat

As a main heating source, electric heat has many disadvantages despite its widespread use:

Increased Operating Costs: Maintaining an electric furnace can be costly.

Health Concerns with Dry Heat: People who have allergies or respiratory problems may find it difficult to cope with the dry heat produced by electric furnaces.

Power Outage Vulnerability: In locations where power outages are common, backup heat sources could be required.

The Distinctions Between Electric and Oil

Regional preferences differ in terms of heating. Even if heating oil is utilized more frequently in the Northeast, it is important to contrast the two systems:

Oil and Electric Furnaces: A Comparison

Because oil furnaces can produce higher temperatures, they work well in colder climates. Furthermore, oil heating offers more durable warmth than electric heat.

Comparing Costs

Homes that use heating oil experience prolonged warmth, and oil heat turns out to be less expensive than electric heat. In areas where winters are harsh, heating oil systems are always a better option.

Choosing the Proper Heating System

The best heating system for your house may depend on a number of things, including where you live. The main points are outlined as follows:

Oil vs. Gas Heat: In comparison to natural gas furnaces, oil heat systems have a longer lifespan and produce more heat.

Oil Heating vs. Electric Heat: Heating oil furnaces generate more heat than electric heat systems, which are typically more expensive to run.

A radiant heating system: what is it?

Do you think about updating your home's radiant heating system? You've arrived at the ideal location.

We'll go over the various kinds of contemporary radiant heating systems, their benefits and drawbacks, and installation costs.

Radiant heating: what is it?

Heat is immediately transferred through a room's ceiling, floors, and walls by a radiant heating system. Convection is the method by which the heated air rises and heats the entire space.

Compared to central heating systems, radiant heating systems offer the following advantages:

- Why Since ducting leaks and holes waste 20–30% of the air in a central heating system, radiant heating is more energy-efficient.
- Your utility bills may go down as a result of radiant heating's decreased energy waste.

- Distinct heating systems are available. There are no vents, air handlers, or grilles can be seen.
- Because radiant heating systems don't have fans or compressors, they run silently.
- Indoor air quality is unaffected by radiant heating.
- Radiant heating systems require less upkeep after installation.
- Contemporary smart thermostats work in tandem with hydronic and electric floor heating systems.

Systems that use radiant heating

Radiant heating systems use a variety of heat sources, such as solar-powered boilers and water heaters. Certain types can also be used as summertime air conditioners.

Radiating air-heated floors

Underfloor ducting is used in air-heated radiant floors. Warm air flows down the duct. The heat is conducted by a concrete slab that is situated between the flooring and the ducts. The room warms up gradually as the air rises.

Radiant flooring with air heating are not prevalent. Air-heated floors are less economical than electric and hydronic radiant floors because of the ductwork.

Radiant floor heating systems

An electrical wire network is used in electric radiant floors. Under flooring that has a large surface area and powerful heat transfer, such ceramic tile, the wires are placed.

For restrooms and other tiny spaces, electric radiant flooring is frequently utilized as an additional heating source. Applications for the entire house are rare because hydronic heating is more economical than electric heating.

Electric radiant flooring is a wise option for existing homes or retrofit situations. In order to save the installation time, many HVAC specialists attach the wires to plastic matting.

Radiant hydronic flooring

Water-filled tubes are used in a network to provide hydronic radiant flooring. The water is heated by a boiler or water heater.

Radiant heating for the entire house is achieved using hydronic radiant floors. It is convenient to have zoned heating when each room has its own temperature control.

Numerous types of flooring are compatible with hydronic heating. There are several options: carpet, concrete, hardwood, and laminate.

Hydronic heating pipes are typically placed in newly constructed homes due to their intrusive and expensive installation. Retrofit application is still practical and secure.

Wall-mounted radiant heating panels

Slabs with hydronic tubes or electrical wires along them are known as radiant heating panels. The bottom four feet of the wall are where the panels are mounted.

An excellent choice for a retrofit in an existing house are radiant wall panels. Radiant floor heating requires more time and money for installation, but it takes less time.

Walls with thick radiant heating panels may protrude outward. Look for panels that are less than an inch thick to reduce any variations in wall depth.

Ceiling-mounted radiant heating panels

It is also possible to install radiant heating panels in ceilings. Electric or hydronic heat sources are used by the panels.

When the outside temperature rises, hydronic ceiling heaters can also be used as cooling systems. Simply fill the tubes with cool water. After rising and coming into contact with the cool ceiling, warm inside air will descend as cool air.

Installing a radiant heating system

Installing radiant heating systems requires a large time commitment. Applications for floors and retrofits can be intrusive, needing more than sixteen man hours.

We advise leaving installation to a qualified expert. Major structural modifications to the house include tearing up the flooring and tearing down the drywall.

How is floor heating that is powered installed?

A lot of experts fasten the electrical cords to a collection of plastic matting. Installations for a single room can be finished in a matter of hours, but it might take several days for the new flooring to dry.

These general procedures are what your HVAC specialist will do:

- If the flooring is retrofit, remove it now.
- Spread a little amount of mortar over the subflooring.
- Place fiberglass insulation batts over the mortar.
- Secure the plastic mats and cords with glue or staples.
- Attach the cables or mats to the electrical wiring in your house.
- Place a leveling compound and flooring (typically ceramic tile) on top of the cables.

How is floor heating with hydronics installed?

A plumber is needed to connect the water tubes to the heat source for hydronic heating. Every radiant-heated floor requires the installer to have access to the ceiling underneath it. This is a simple technique with unfinished homes. It might be necessary for the installer to pull down drywall if you're retrofitting.

This general procedure is followed by the installer and plumber:

- Draw a schematic of the tubing arrangement beneath the floor. (They require access to the ceiling because of this.)
- To provide space for the tubes, drill holes in the floor joists.
- Place the tubes in and secure them with staples to the floor's underside.
- Place insulation batts over the tubes.
- Attach the tubes to the boiler or water heater.
- Install flooring above the tubes and level the surface.

The typical time to install 1,000 square feet of tubing is 8 to 16 hours. Retrofits can take longer, while new home installation is at the lower end of that spectrum.

How are panels for radiant heating installed?

Installing radiant heating panels is less complicated than floor heating. The expert takes the following four actions:

- Take down the sheetrock or drywall.
- Put the panel in place.
- Insulate the wall or ceiling on one or both sides.
- Put the sheetrock or drywall back in place.

Each room typically takes one to three hours to install. Installing panels on ceilings takes longer than on walls.

Consult your HVAC specialist to verify the location of the panels before fastening artwork or mirrors to a completed wall. Although it might vary, panels are typically installed in the lower four feet of the wall.

Radiant heating costs

Installing radiant heating requires more than just time investment. Radiant heating systems can be expensive initially due to high labor costs. Still, the energy savings can make it beneficial.

The HomeAdvisor-provided cost information below represents national averages.

Radiant floor heating costs

The average cost of hydronic floor heating is $13 per square foot. Because water is a powerful heat conductor, hydronic floor heating is less expensive to run than electric floor heating.

Hydronic heating is more expensive overall because of the water source. A water heater can be purchased for $300–2,000, and installation can go from $770 to $1,450. A typical boiler unit costs approximately $3,000, with installation costing between $3,500 and $7,700.

The average cost of electric heating is $11/square foot. Operating a 100 square foot space requires an average daily energy expenditure of $1–5. Compared to electricity, hydronic heating is less expensive.

The average cost to lay flooring over your heating system is as follows:

Material	Cost per square foot	Recommended rooms
Ceramic tile	$20-40	Bathrooms
Concrete	$15-30	Basements, garages
Laminate/hardwood	$15-20	Kitchens, living rooms

The price of radiant floor panels

At $50–60 per square foot, radiant heating panels are less expensive than wires or tubes. Typically, panels are 2' x 2' or 2' x 6' in size.

Most rooms require one or two ceiling or wall panels. The entire cost per room, including materials and labor, is between $300 and $1,400.

How to Safeguard Yourself Against Common HVAC Scams

The majority of HVAC contractors are reputable, hardworking individuals who make substantial contributions to their neighborhood by providing necessary heating and cooling services. However, there are some rotten apples in every sector.

Concern over HVAC scams that take unsuspecting homes by surprise is growing. Here at HVAC.com, your go-to resource for anything HVAC, we're here to help you stay safe by illuminating the most prevalent HVAC scams. Avoid becoming a victim of dishonest professionals who are out to get a quick profit; instead, be knowledgeable and safeguard both your house and your finances.

Typical HVAC Frauds and How to Spot Them

Overspending on Labor and Parts

You're not the only one who had sticker shock when you saw your most recent HVAC bill. Inflating the cost of components and labor for homeowners is one of the most prevalent HVAC scams. This usually happens when the amount on the final invoice differs from the amount that was originally quoted. Scammy professionals could put on extra fees, report unanticipated problems, or inflate the price of new parts.

Avoid this HVAC fraud by always requesting a written estimate in detail and thorough documentation of any modifications made during the service.

Deals That Seem Too Good to Be True

If something sounds too good to be true, it usually is, just like everything else in life! A warning light should be raised if an HVAC contractor provides an incredibly low service charge or makes large savings on the installation or repairs of HVAC equipment. These seeming too good to be true offers are used by con artists to entice homeowners to accept their offer.

Advice on how to prevent falling for this HVAC scam: Make sure you get a documented agreement that details all services and prices.

Unsuitable Replacement of Components

Unreliable HVAC experts may advise replacing functional parts prematurely, which would dramatically increase the cost of repairs. Only HVAC technicians can access expensive HVAC parts like an air conditioner compressor or furnace heat exchanger, thus homeowners are at the mercy of their advice.

Advice on how to avoid falling for this HVAC scam includes getting a detailed explanation before authorizing any part replacement and, if need, getting a second opinion from a reliable HVAC specialist.

Replace System Immediately

An HVAC contractor should always be avoided if they insist on replacing your system right away, especially if a repair would be just as effective. Rather than having to spend several hundred dollars on a straightforward repair, you might have to pay over $10,000 for a full system replacement.

Advice on avoiding this HVAC scam: Before making a major replacement purchase, always get a second opinion. Something can be wrong if two technicians give assessments that are noticeably different from one another.

Misrepresenting a Reputable Company

Posing as a representative of a reputable HVAC company, an HVAC scammer can come to your house and offer a free inspection. This is a common strategy used by these kinds of impostors as a springboard for other fraudulent acts.

Advice on how to prevent falling for this HVAC scam: Never take up unsolicited offers from strangers. Always check the company they work for and their credentials. Make sure they are wearing or driving a car with the company's logo.

Superfluous Inspections

Although routine HVAC maintenance and inspections are essential for spotting possible problems, some businesses could try to upsell needless inspections.

Advice on how to prevent falling for this HVAC scam: Be wary of cold-calling HVAC companies that promise free inspections; they can be con artists. Once more, if something seems too good to be true, it probably is.

Always Pressing for a Greater System Size

In terms of HVAC systems, bigger isn't always better. The capacity of an air conditioning and heating system, not its actual size, is what is meant by its size. Certain contractors may insist on installing a larger unit because they say it will run more smoothly.

This is a problem for a number of reasons. First of all, installing an HVAC system that is too large for your room might result in short cycling, higher wear and tear, and expensive energy bills. In addition, problems with humidity may arise from an enormous HVAC system. This occurs when a system that is too big for your house cools it down too quickly without properly clearing the air of extra humidity. Regrettably, replacing an outdated HVAC system is the only way to address an incorrectly sized system.

Advice on avoiding this HVAC scam: To find out what size system is best for your house, demand a Manual J load estimate from a reputable HVAC professional.

Supplying Rechargeable AC Refrigerant

You're probably being duped if an HVAC contractor recommends refilling the AC refrigerant without taking care of the underlying problem. Recharging your air conditioner is probably a sign that there is a refrigerant leak that needs to be fixed.

How to avoid falling for this HVAC scam: Steer clear of HVAC contractors who suggest recharging without first identifying the source of the problem or presenting evidence of a refrigerant leak.

Unclean Filter Lie

In an attempt to pull off the "dirty filter" scam, some con artists pose as homeowners and show them a filter they brought with them, saying it was actually from their apartment. They might market pricey air filtration or quality treatment devices by using this deceit.

Advice on how to prevent falling for this popular HVAC scam is to educate yourself on how to check and replace your HVAC air filter.

Air Duct Cleaning Frauds

In the HVAC sector, there is a frequent discussion about how often air duct cleaning should be done. Your ducts are concealed from view, therefore scammers that offer frequent duct cleaning services can take advantage of this lack of visibility. Some dishonest HVAC providers would advise routine air duct cleaning, citing serious health risks and charging absurdly low prices for the procedure. These con artists can leave the ducts in worse shape or don't do any maintenance at all.

The Environmental Protection Agency advises just cleaning air ducts when necessary, not on a regular basis. Instances like mold growth or bug infestations may call for air duct cleaning.

Avoid this HVAC fraud by insisting that the HVAC firm provide documentation—such as video shots from their initial ductwork inspection—proving that your air ducts require cleaning.

Advice for Selecting an HVAC Firm

The best defense against falling for an HVAC scam is due diligence on the part of the prospective client and hiring a reliable HVAC professional. Think about selecting an HVAC business that has received good reviews on websites like Angi, Yelp, and Google Reviews. Another useful tool for choosing which company to hire and which ones to avoid is the Better Business Bureau.

Make sure they have the right insurance in case of any unanticipated accidents or damage to your house, and ask them to show documentation of any licenses and certificates that they may need in your area. Additionally, confirm that the business has liability and worker's compensation insurance.

You usually can't go wrong with an HVAC firm that has a lengthy history of delivering service in your area, even when younger businesses could give outstanding service. These businesses frequently employ seasoned experts with years of experience in the field who are qualified to identify difficult problems and fix a wide range of systems.

What Is A Heat Pump

Describe a heat pump, please. An outdoor heat pump is a component of a residential air conditioning and heating system. It may provide heat as well as cool your house, much like a central air conditioner can. A heat pump takes heat from the chilly exterior air into your home during the cooler months and removes heat from your home during the warmer months in order to cool it. They use refrigerant to convey heat and are powered by electricity, so they can be comfortable all year round.

It's possible that homeowners won't need to build separate systems to heat their homes because they manage both cooling and heating. An electric heat strip can be fitted to the interior fan coil for further functionality in colder climates. Heat pumps are more environmentally friendly than furnaces because they don't burn fossil fuels.

WHICH HEAT PUMP TYPES ARE THERE?

Ground-source and air-source heat pumps are the two most used varieties. More often used for home heating and cooling, air-source heat pumps transfer heat from indoor to outdoor air.

Geothermal heat pumps, also known as ground-source heat pumps, move heat from the earth outside of your house into the air inside of it. Due to the same ground temperature throughout the year, these require a higher initial cost but are usually more efficient and have lower running costs.

HOW ARE HEAT PUMPS OPERATED?

How are heat pumps operated? Heat pumps use various air or heat sources to move heat from one location to another. Whereas ground source heat pumps, also referred to as geothermal heat pumps, carry heat from a house's interior to its exterior, air source heat pumps move heat from a house's interior to its exterior. The basic operation of both is the same, but we will concentrate on air source heat pumps.

ESSENTIAL HEAT PUMPS

Although they carry heat from one location to another, heat pumps do not produce heat. A heat pump transmits heat energy from the outside air to the interior air, even in freezing temperatures, while a furnace generates heat that is distributed throughout a house. Both an air conditioner and a heat pump work in the same way when they are in cooling mode, taking heat from the inside air and expelling it via the exterior unit.

The size of the house and the temperature in the area are two crucial considerations when deciding which kind of system is appropriate for your house.

WHERE ARE HEAT PUMPS MOST EFFECTIVE?

Before investing in a heat pump system, homeowners in need of new heating or cooling equipment would want to think about the kind of climate they reside in. In milder areas, when the temperature rarely drops below freezing, heat pumps are more prevalent. They can also be used in conjunction with furnaces in colder climates to provide energy-efficient warmth on all but the coldest days. The system will use the furnace to provide heat when the outdoor temperature drops too much for the heat pump to function properly. This type of system, which is incredibly economical and energy efficient, is frequently referred to as a dual fuel system.

Key elements of a heat pump system

An interior air handler unit and an outdoor unit, which resembles the outside unit of a split-system air conditioning system, are the two main parts of a typical air source heat pump system. Numerous significant sub-components are present in both the indoor and outdoor units.

OUTSIDE ROOM

There is a coil and a fan in the outdoor unit. When in cooling mode, the coil functions as a condenser; when in heating mode, it functions as an evaporator. The heat exchange is facilitated by the fan blowing outside air over the coil.

INTERNAL UNIT

The inside unit, also known as the air handler unit, has a coil and a fan just like the outdoor unit. In cooling mode, the coil functions as an evaporator; in heating mode, it functions as a condenser. Air must be circulated throughout the home's ducts and across the coil by the fan.

AIR-RESISTANT

The material that moves through the heat pump system, absorbing and rejecting heat, is called refrigerant.

CONTENSOR

The refrigerant is pressurized and circulated throughout the system by the compressor.

GROUNDING VALVE

The component of the heat pump system that flips the refrigerant flow so that the system can function in the opposite way and alternate between heating and cooling.

HYPERVENTION VALVE

By controlling the flow of the refrigerant through the system, the expansion valve serves as a metering device and permits a drop in the temperature and pressure of the refrigerant.

HOW COOL AND HEAT IS A HEAT PUMP WORKING?

Heat is not produced by heat pumps. They use a refrigerant that circulates between the outdoor compressor and the indoor fan coil (air handler) unit to transfer heat from the earth or the air.

A heat pump discharges heat outdoors while it is in cooling mode, absorbing heat within your house. When the heat pump is in the heating mode, it draws heat from the earth and outside air—even chilly air—and transfers it inside.

The operation of a heat pump in cooling mode

Heat energy naturally seeks to migrate to regions with lower temperatures and lower pressure, which makes it one of the most crucial concepts to grasp about heat pump operation and the process of transferring heat. Heat pumps use this physical characteristic to naturally transfer heat by bringing it into contact with environments that are colder and have lower pressure. This is the operation of a heat pump.

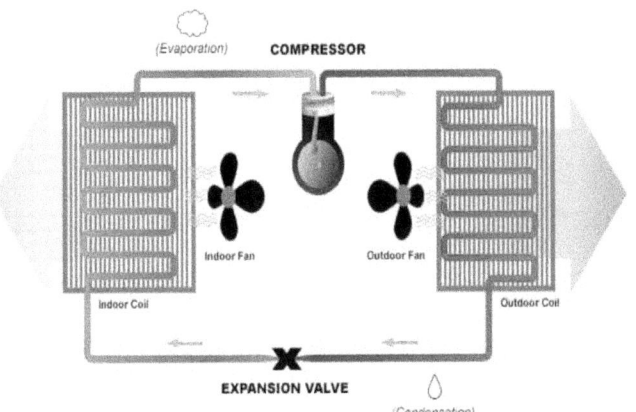

STEP 1

The indoor coil, which serves as the evaporator, has an expansion device that pumps liquid refrigerant through it. The refrigerant absorbs heat energy on the coils when air from within the house is blown across them. The resulting cool air is circulated via the ducts in the house. The liquid refrigerant has heated up and evaporated into gas form as a result of absorbing the heat energy.

STEP 2

After going through a compressor, the gaseous refrigerant is now pressurized. The gas heats up during the pressurization process (a physical feature of compressed gases). The system transports the heated, pressurized refrigerant to the coil located in the outdoor unit.

Step 3

When the outdoor unit is in cooling mode, the coils act as condenser coils, and a fan drives air from the outside across them. Heat is transmitted from the heated compressed gas refrigerant in the coil to the outside air because the air outside the house is colder than the inside air. The refrigerant cools throughout this process and condenses back into a liquid state. Pumped through the system to the expansion valve at the indoor units is the heated liquid refrigerant.

Step 4

The expansion valve considerably lowers the warm liquid refrigerant's pressure, causing it to cool. At this stage, the refrigerant is liquid and cool, ready to be pumped back to the indoor unit's evaporator coil to restart the cycle.

HEATING MODE: THE WORKS OF A HEAT PUMP

When in heating mode, a heat pump functions similarly to that in cooling mode, with the exception that the appropriately titled reversing valve reverses the refrigerant flow. Even in cold weather, the heating source changes to the outside air due to flow reversal, which releases heat energy within the house. The inside coil now serves as the condenser, and the exterior coil serves as the evaporator.

The procedure follows the same laws of physics. Cool liquid refrigerant in the outdoor unit absorbs heat energy and transforms it into chilly gas. After that, pressure is added to the cold gas to transform it into hot gas. By moving air through the device indoors, heating it, and condensing the hot gas to warm liquid, the heated gas is cooled. As the warm liquid enters the outdoor unit, pressure is released, converting it to cold liquid and restarting the cycle.

INSTALATION OF A HEAT PUMP

It can be difficult to install a heat pump; you'll need to have a solid understanding of electrical connections and HVAC systems. The complexity of the installation procedure highlights how crucial it is to entrust the work to a professional. Your neighborhood Carrier specialist has the skills, background, and understanding required to guarantee a smooth and effective installation. They evaluate each space's unique needs for heating and cooling before precisely measuring and arranging the heat pump. They carefully arrange and carry out the installation, taking into account things like ducting, electrical compatibility, and best location. Giving the installation to a Carrier specialist guarantees not only a heat pump that operates as intended but also piece of mind due to the system's precise and safety standard-abiding installation.

OVERVIEW OF THE WORKS OF A HEAT PUMP

Heat pumps are adaptable, effective heating and cooling devices. A reversing valve allows a heat pump to alter the refrigerant flow, which can heat or cool a house. An evaporator coil is covered in air, which transfers heat energy from the air to the refrigerant. The refrigerant circulates the heat energy to a condenser coil, where a fan blows air across the coil to release it. Heat is transferred between locations using this mechanism.

Chapter 4

The Importance Of Proper Ventilation In Commercial And Industrial Buildings

Appropriate ventilation has grown in significance in commercial and industrial buildings in recent years. Many nations have laws and regulations requiring employers to provide proper ventilation, particularly in cases where hazardous or dangerous situations exist. However, firms should take into account the comfort of their employees, energy economy, and air quality in addition to merely adhering to the law when it comes to ventilation.

This book explores the significance of adequate ventilation in commercial and industrial buildings, outlining ways in which companies can provide a comfortable, energy-efficient, and healthy work environment for their staff. We'll examine the many kinds of ventilation systems and consider how to make ventilation better. We'll also discuss the possible advantages of adequate ventilation for the long-term viability of the company.

Businesses can save energy expenses and protect the health and safety of their staff by implementing an effective ventilation strategy. Now let's explore the significance of appropriate ventilation for commercial and industrial buildings and learn how companies can maximize their ventilation system.

How Appropriate Ventilation Can Help To Maintain Good Air Quality

- Types of Industrial and Commercial Building Ventilation Systems
- The Advantages Of Adequate Ventilation
- Typical Problems Linked to Inadequate Ventilation
- Ways To Increase Ventilation In Commercial And Industrial Structures
- Final Thoughts

Types of Industrial and Commercial Building Ventilation Systems

Any business or industrial facility must have ventilation systems since they are in charge of giving the occupants of the area clean, healthy air to breathe. Maintaining pleasant temperatures, lowering energy expenses, and lowering indoor air pollution are all made possible by proper ventilation. For commercial and industrial buildings, there are various types of ventilation systems available, each having advantages and disadvantages of their own.

1. **Forced Air System:** The most popular kind of ventilation system, the forced air system circulates air throughout the building using an air handler. Because this system is simple to install

and maintain, it is commonly seen in commercial and industrial structures. The drawback of this kind of system is that it might be costly to run because frequent operation of the air handler is required to maintain enough airflow.

2. **Natural Ventilation System:** Utilizing natural air movement to introduce fresh air into the building, the natural ventilation system is an additional type of ventilation system. Since this system is an affordable means of ensuring proper ventilation, industrial buildings are usually the ones that use it. The air quality might change according on the ambient temperature and humidity, which is a drawback of this method.

3. **Mechanical Ventilation System:** Utilizing a fan to circulate air throughout the building, this type of system is the final one. Since this technique is more efficient than forced air, it is commonly utilized in commercial buildings. This system's drawback is that it needs more upkeep than the other two kinds of systems.

Ensuring adequate airflow is crucial regardless of the type of ventilation system being utilized. Maintaining pleasant temperatures, lowering energy expenses, and lowering indoor air pollution are all made possible by proper ventilation. Commercial and industrial facilities may guarantee a safe and healthy environment for their occupants by investing in the appropriate kind of system.

Advantages Of Adequate Ventilation

Adequate ventilation is a critical component of any commercial or industrial building. It assists in regulating the building's humidity and temperature in addition to guaranteeing the workers' health and safety. In addition to improving worker breathing, proper ventilation also helps to lower the quantity of dust, debris, and other pollutants in the air.

Appropriate ventilation in a business or industrial facility has numerous advantages. The following are some of the main benefits:

1. **It enhances the quality** of the air by removing dust and other particles, which makes the air safer and healthier to breathe. It can also aid in maintaining the building's humidity and temperature at a comfortable level, which will improve the working environment.

2. **It lessens moisture and mold growth:** Inadequate ventilation can make the air stagnant, which can raise the humidity level in the space. This may promote the formation of mildew and mold, which could endanger the health of the workers. An effective ventilation system lowers this risk.
3. **It lowers energy expenses**: A building's temperature can be regulated with proper ventilation, requiring less effort from the heating or air conditioning system. As a result, there can be a decrease in energy expenses.
4. **It can aid in increasing productivity:** Since employees are not subjected to uncomfortable temperatures or poor air quality, good ventilation can aid in increasing concentration. A rise in productivity may result from this.

In conclusion, having enough ventilation in commercial and industrial buildings has a lot of advantages. Appropriate ventilation can significantly affect a business's long-term profitability by lowering energy costs, enhancing productivity, and supplying healthy air quality.

Common Issues Associated With Poor Ventilation

In commercial and industrial buildings, inadequate ventilation can be a serious problem that causes a variety of issues. For the people who work or visit these places to be safe, healthy, and comfortable, adequate ventilation is essential. The following are some of the most typical problems brought on by inadequate ventilation:

1. **Low Air Quality:** Inadequate ventilation can result in lower air quality, which can have negative health effects. Fatigue, headaches, respiratory issues, and general discomfort can all be brought on by poor air quality.

2. **Mold and mildew:** Inadequate ventilation can raise the humidity, which fosters the growth of mold and mildew. This can cause damage to structures, furnishings, and equipment and can occur both indoors and outdoors.
3. **Odors:** Bad odors can accumulate in a place due to inadequate ventilation, creating an unpleasant atmosphere. Employee productivity may suffer as a result, and health complaints may rise.
4. **Uncomfortable Working circumstances:** Inadequate ventilation can cause a room to become excessively hot or chilly, which can lead to uncomfortable living or working circumstances. Additionally, because sound can become trapped, it may exacerbate noise issues.

Commercial and industrial facilities must have adequate ventilation to preserve a safe and healthy atmosphere. To make sure ventilation systems are operating correctly, it's critical to do routine maintenance and inspections. A well-designed ventilation system can lessen the possibility of unpleasant working conditions, property damage, and health issues.

Ways To Increase Ventilation In Commercial And Industrial Structures

To protect the health and safety of building occupants, commercial and industrial facilities must improve their ventilation systems. The amounts of humidity, airborne pollutants, and other dangerous materials can be decreased with the use of proper ventilation. The following are some ideas to enhance ventilation in business and industrial buildings:

1. **Install Energy-Efficient Ventilation Systems:** Adding energy-efficient ventilation systems improves ventilation and lowers building operating expenses. These systems make use of sensors to determine the temperature and modify the ventilation as necessary.
2. **Use Natural Ventilation:** By drawing in outside air and pushing out stale air, natural ventilation helps to lower energy usage and improve air quality. Installing intake and exhaust fans or opening windows and doors can accomplish this.
3. **Make Use of HVAC Systems:** HVAC systems (heating, ventilation, and air conditioning) ensure adequate ventilation and appropriate interior

temperatures. Air quality and the operation of the ventilation system are guaranteed by well-maintained HVAC systems.

4. **Upgrading air filters** on a regular basis can help cut down on the quantity of dust, pollen, and other particles in the air. This lowers the chance of health issues and enhances indoor air quality.

Commercial and industrial buildings can enhance their ventilation and protect the health and safety of their occupants by using the above-mentioned methods. Ensuring a comfortable and healthy interior environment requires adequate ventilation.

Final Thoughts On The Value Of Adequate Ventilation

Because of the many dangerous chemicals and particles that exist in commercial and industrial buildings, proper ventilation is crucial. Inadequate ventilation can lower the building's air quality, making the circumstances uncomfortable and even dangerous for the people and animals who use it.

It's crucial to keep in mind that not every ventilation system is created equal when it comes to adequate ventilation. The capabilities and advantages of various ventilation system types can influence a building's air quality.

It is impossible to exaggerate how crucial adequate ventilation is to keeping any structure or place of employment safe and healthy. It can lessen the likelihood of accidents and health problems brought on by poor air quality in addition to helping to remove pollutants and maintain clean air. In addition to lowering employee stress and weariness, proper ventilation can lower the risk of fire from blocked ducts and other issues.

Main components of a ventilation system

Having examined the primary system types now in use, it is now appropriate to delve deeper into the various components of a ventilation system and their respective functions.

Filter

When we discuss the filter, we are discussing one of the most important parts of a ventilation system. Its primary purpose is to keep all kinds of particles—dust, filth, insects, and so on—out of the areas that need to be ventilated.

The quality of the air coming in from the outside and the air we wish to bring inside will determine the kind of filter that should be utilized.

Heat pumps, electric resistances, or hot water batteries

Its purpose is to keep extremely cold air from entering the house and causing discomfort. The air is heated by these elements until the desired temperature is reached in the space.

Coil for cooling

By cooling the air that enters from the outside to a suitable temperature, this component performs the opposite function of electrical resistances. Though there are other varieties, direct expansion and cold water systems are the most frequently utilized.

Heat restoration

Heat recovery is the most effective air treatment technique in terms of energy usage. Its simple mechanism recovers up to 90% of the sensible heat from exhaust air by transferring heat (or cold, in summer) from the exhaust air to the intake air with only one fan's energy consumption.

Dehumidifiers or humidifiers

They are a feature that we are finding more and more often, even though they are not found in every system. They are employed to increase and decrease the humidity content of the surrounding air until more suitable levels are reached. Hospitals and medical facilities may find it useful for antibacterial treatment, among its other applications.

The Basics Of Air Filtration In HVAC Design

Do you have an HVAC system in your building? It probably does. However, does that imply that the interior air quality for your building's tenants is adequate or even acceptable? It is rather likely that it doesn't. However, why is this relevant?

We will examine the variations in HVAC systems' air filtering capacities, the reasons behind these variations' substantial influence on indoor air quality, and the multiple implications these variations have for buildings, their proprietors, and their inhabitants.

An HVAC system: What Is It?

Almost every public building has a basic air filtering system called HVAC (Heating, Ventilation, and Air Conditioning). These air handling systems are designed to fulfill a very broad purpose: to offer acceptable indoor air quality derived from appropriate ventilation that includes (to varied extents) air filtration and maintaining comfortable indoor air temperature.

But not all HVAC systems are the same. The air filtering component of HVAC systems is widely variable. The many methods of filtration, types, and ratings of filters used in HVAC systems are vital to how efficient they are in cleaning the air throughout the HVAC system and, in turn, their impact on a building and its occupants.

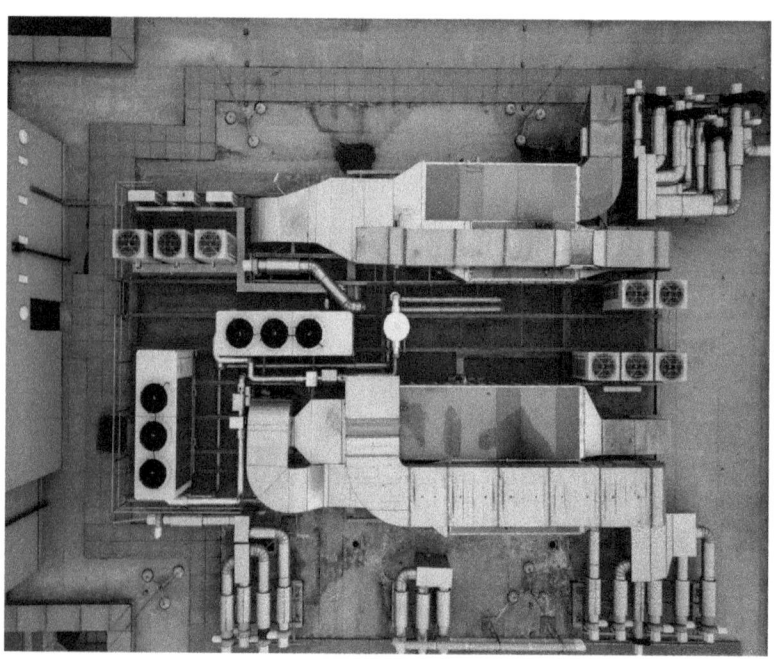

How Air Filtration Is Integrated Within HVAC Systems

Originally air filtering devices in an HVAC system were put in place to avoid dust accumulation off heating and cooling coils. They have since evolved to accommodate the changing demands of schools, companies, and other building tenants.

While most HVAC systems still feature basic degrees of air filtration, which can trap air born particulate and pollutants. Manufacturers have made tweaks, and enhancements to existing designs, and new technologies have permitted the development of systems that can minimize or remove airborne contaminants.

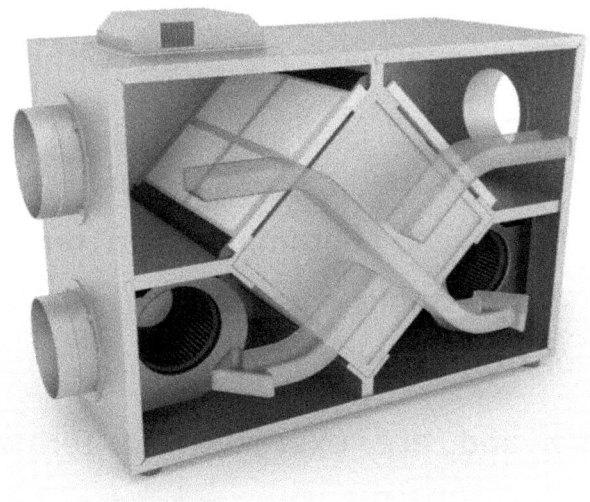

What Airborne Contaminants Do HVAC Systems Remove?

There are numerous of pollutants and particulate that can be detected within buildings. Contaminants discovered in building HVAC systems can be divided into three broad categories:

1. Particulate (dust, filth, smoke, etc.) The most frequent kind of airborne stuff.
2. gases, including sulfur dioxide, carbon monoxide, nitrogen oxide, and ozone. The majority of these enter the building through the fresh air intake of the HVAC system, although others may enter by off-gassing from synthetic materials within the structure.
3. Biological (including fungi, viruses, and bacteria). These are the tiniest contaminants in terms of particles, and they might enter the structure from the outside or from within.

Particle sizes vary and are expressed in terms of micrometers, or microns. For instance, dirt has a diameter of several thousand microns, yet gaseous pollutants often have a diameter of less than 0.01 microns. An HVAC system's proper air filtering is required to successfully lower the quantity of pollutants inside buildings.

In order to establish an objective classification system based on how well an air filtering system eliminates or lowers certain particulates, ASHRAE (The American Society of Heating, Refrigerating and Air-Conditioning Engineers) created a standard for testing filters. This standard is used to rate all filters, which range from 1 to 20. The degree of filtration improves with a higher MERV rating.

It's not always the case that a higher MERV rating is better for your building. The higher ratings may indicate more effective filtration, but they also increase airflow resistance in the system, which needs to be countered by rebalancing the system and using more fan energy. This may result in a significant increase in your overall energy costs. Building managers should therefore be aware of the possibilities and the appropriate type of filter for their particular building.

Why Is Air Filtration Important for HVAC Systems?

Effective air filtration greatly benefits all public buildings' occupants, as the quality of the air inside them has a direct impact on them.

Poor air quality can be one of the biggest workplace hazards, from the transmission of common winter viruses that can swiftly infect schools and offices to facilitating the spread of germs, dust, mildew, volatile organic compounds, and other toxins.

Ignorance of air quality in an environment can exacerbate or exacerbate health issues like asthma and allergies. Inadequate indoor air quality can raise the risk of illness among residents, which can lead to a rise in sick days and decreased attendance. Research has demonstrated that low levels of indoor air quality can cause cognitive impairment, which includes delayed reaction times, poor decision-making, and other productivity-related issues. Additionally, there is proof that poor indoor air quality negatively impacts mental health.

If a building doesn't provide good indoor air quality, which is increasingly seen as a basic need, building owners may have more difficulty finding tenants. In addition to adding to the building's longevity and structural integrity, which makes investing in air filtration a prudent financial decision over the long run, superior air filtration attracts tenants by safeguarding their health and enhancing their own business.

How To Select Your Building's Ideal Air Filtration System

The choice of air filtration system that is best for your HVAC system will depend on a number of criteria, including the building's architecture, interior volume, and usage, as well as whether a permanent or flexible solution is required. Air exchanges per hour (ACH) and cubic feet per minute (CFM) are two examples of efficiency metrics that are taken into account.

Chapter 5

The Refrigeration Cycle

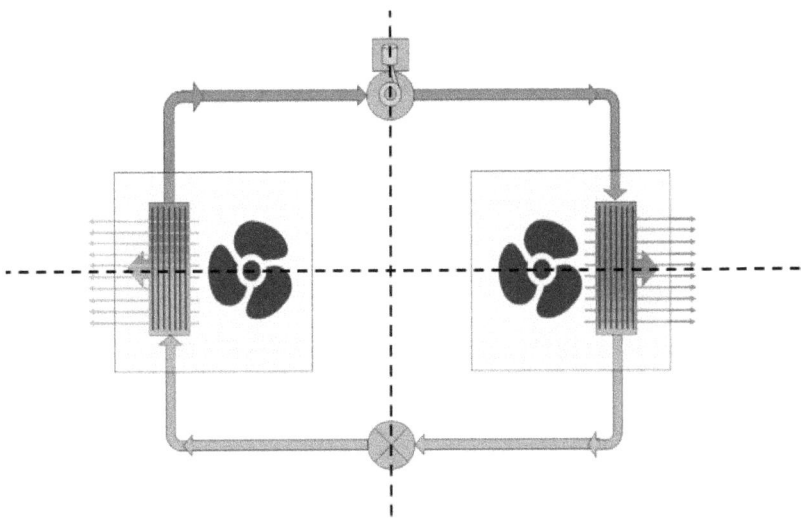

The refrigeration cycle is a basic yet remarkably intelligent and practical mechanism.

The refrigeration cycle requires only four fundamental components to complete the circuit in its most basic form:

- The Compressor
- A cooling unit
- A Limitation
- A subcooler

That is all. That's nearly all; in order for the circuit to cycle, we also need a refrigerant.

The process of refrigeration is cyclical, as the term implies.

The cycle begins at the compressor and continues via the condenser, restriction, evaporator, and compressor before returning to the compressor to complete the loop.

So let's take a quick look at each element individually. Fortunately, their names speak for themselves:

1. The Compressor

You may consider the compressor to be the center of the operation.

By compressing the refrigerant gas, it functions as a pump to provide circulation by generating a pressure differential that propels the refrigerant around the circuit continuously.

2. The Condenser

The refrigerant gas from the compressor is cooled and condensed by the condenser into a vapour and then a liquid.

3. The Restriction

The restriction causes a pressure differential between the evaporator and itself while limiting the flow of liquid refrigerant. Since the limitation meters the amount of refrigerant entering the evaporator, it is more generally referred to as a METERING DEVICE.

4. The Evaporator

Before the liquid refrigerant returns to the compressor, the evaporator turns it first into a vapour and then a gas.

5. The Refrigerant

You may have noted that we have previously discussed the refrigerant's characteristics as a GAS, VAPOUR, and LIQUID in this succinct and simplified introduction to the parts. The primary idea of the refrigeration cycle is this change in state within the refrigerant, which creates the refrigeration effect. More on this a little later.

Here are some illustrations of these elements and their appearances:

1. The Compressor

The compressor, which comes in a wide range of sizes, is the central component of the refrigeration cycle.

When there are several compressors used in a big system, they are typically located within a plant room, while in smaller systems, they are typically located inside the outdoor unit.

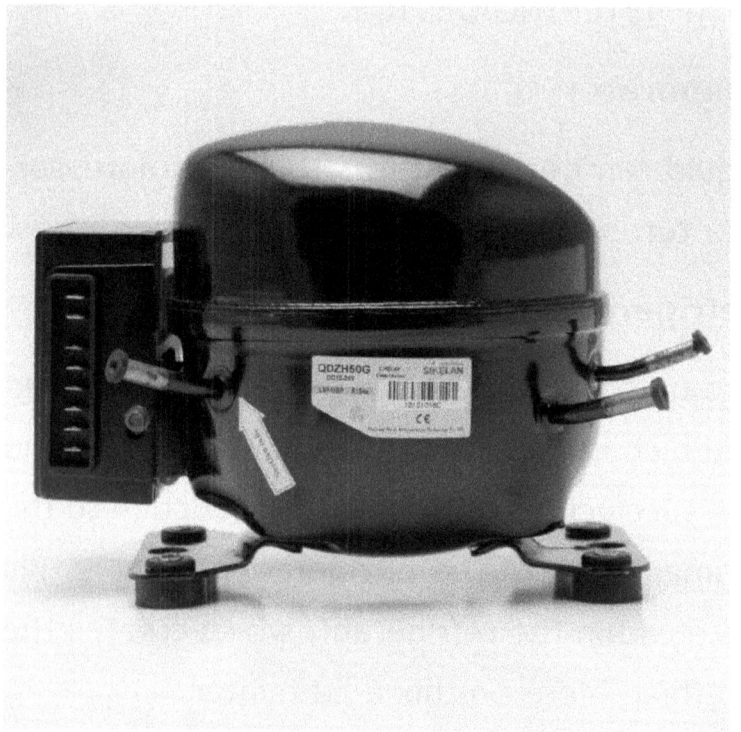

A tiny compressor for pot.

compressors with different capacities.

a substantial compressor rack.

2. The Condenser

The condenser is frequently referred to as the "outdoor unit" since that is typically where it is located—outdoors, fixed to a wall, floor, or roof. In the majority of air conditioning and smaller refrigeration units, the compressor, condenser, many electronics, and occasionally the limitation (metering device) are housed in the exterior unit.

condenser in a cold room.

rooftop condensers for a chiller.

compressors used in air cooling.

3. The Restriction (Metering Instrument).

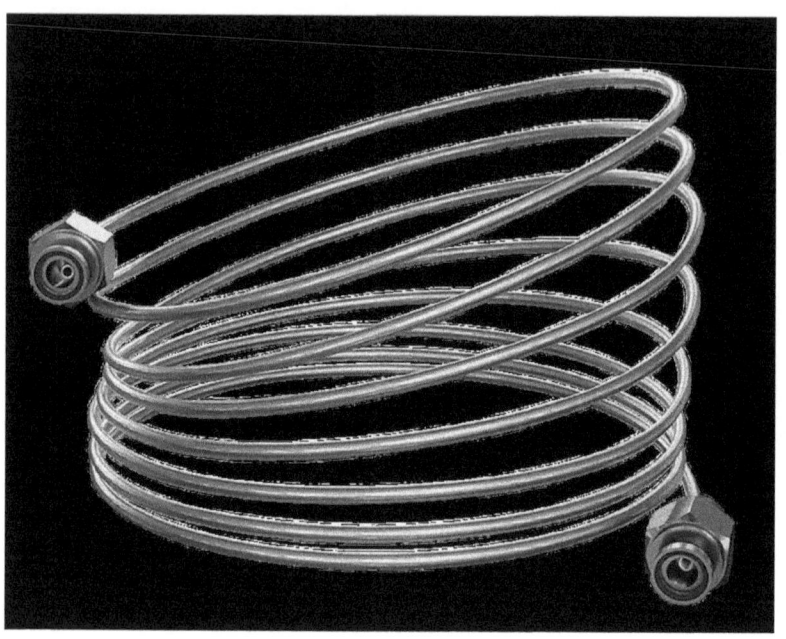

A measuring apparatus for capillaries.

A thermometer kind of meter.

an apparatus for electronic metering.

All modern air conditioning and refrigeration systems will employ one of these three types of metering devices.

Simply said, capillary tubes are very short tubes that obstruct the flow of refrigerant.

The most typical places to find them are on tiny refrigerators, like the ones you have at home.

All refrigeration systems use thermostatic metering devices, often known as thermostatic expansion valves, or TEVs for short. They use a bulb that is tethered to pipework that emerges from the evaporator and is half filled with refrigerant. By using pressure to open and close, this bulb may change the amount of refrigerant entering the evaporator based on the temperature of the refrigerant exiting the evaporator.

A more accurate and contemporary form of a TEV is an electronic metering device, often known as an EEV or EXV (Electronic Expansion Valves). They can open and close several times per second to enable extremely fine control of the amount of refrigerant entering the evaporator. They are electronically controlled using data from an electronic pressure sensor.

The Restriction or Metering Device's function can be roughly compared to that of an aerosol spray can's nozzle to assist understand it.

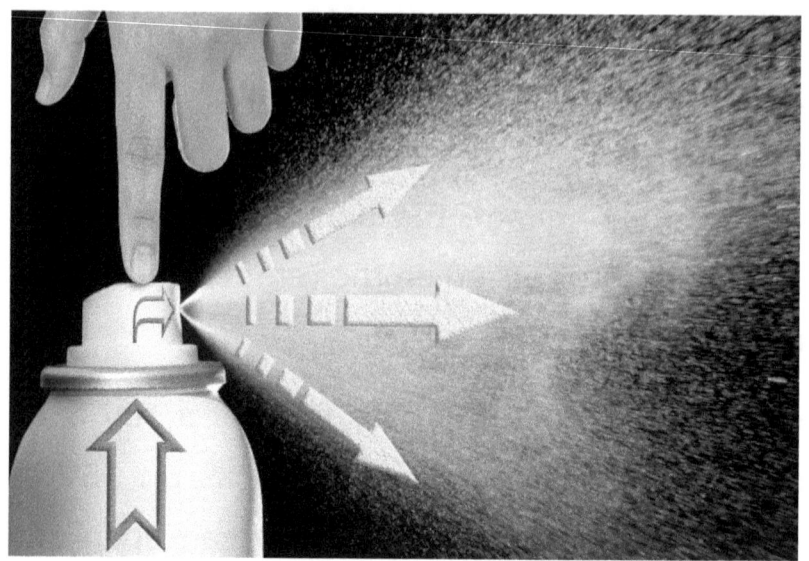

4. The Evaporator

The evaporator is commonly known as the "indoor unit" since that is typically where it is located—inside the space that is being cooled, or heated in the case of heat pump air conditioning. Usually, they are placed high on a wall or ceiling.

Evaporator in a cold room.

an evaporator for air conditioning.

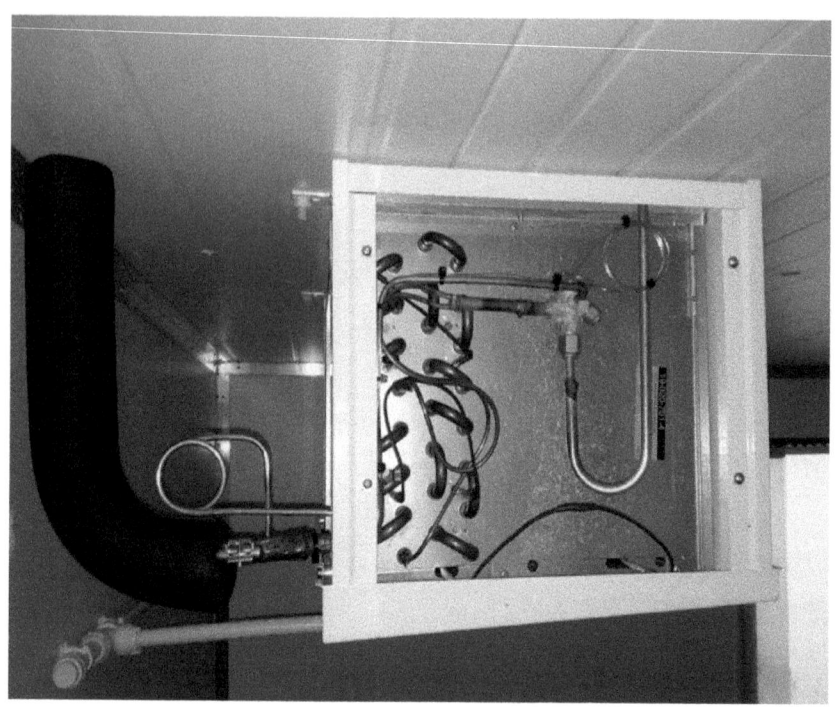

A evaporator in a chiller room.

The construction of the coils in the evaporator and condenser is essentially the same.

a lengthy section of pipework with aluminum fins all around it.

In essence, they are heat exchangers, much like an automobile's radiator.

coils for evaporators.

coils for evaporators. coils for condensers.

5. The Refrigerant

Refrigerants and their blends come in a wide variety of varieties. For example, different refrigerants have distinct qualities for freezers, cold rooms, and air conditioners.

The term "R" number is typically used to identify refrigerants, such as R32, R410A, R422D, and R507.

We currently also utilize CO2 (R744), ammonia (R717), and propane (R290) as refrigerants.

various refrigerants in abundance. in a wide range of sizes.

a sight glass used to view the system's refrigerant level.

It's critical to comprehend what refrigeration genuinely is before moving forward:

Refrigeration is the process of cooling a material, system, or space so that its temperature falls and stays below the surrounding air temperature (while the removed heat is rejected at a higher temperature). To put it another way, refrigeration is artificially produced cooling.

This definition's key component is the "removed heat."

Something that lacks "Heat" is what you consider to be "Cold."

A refrigeration system's only function is to take heat out of places it shouldn't be.

Since heat is subjective, what do you think is hot?

Realizing that heat is relative is crucial to comprehending the refrigeration cycle.

Heat is often associated with circumstances and experiences from our daily lives.

We consider it to be a BLAZING HOT day at 30°C!

Even on that scorching day, it seems very cold as we take a dip in the 16°C sea!

Thus, our sense of heat has changed from BOILING to FREEZING in just 14°C!

However, the reality is completely different when we compare those temps to other temperatures.

Given that the sun's temperature is 5,500°C, our 30°C HOT day seems downright frigid. Similarly, liquid nitrogen at -200°C appears to be blazing hot, despite our frigid 16°C sea!

The first thing that comes to mind when we hear the word "BOILING" is boiling water in a kettle at 100 degrees. Boiling is inherently associated with a temperature of 100°C. It's crucial to realize, though, that this phenomenon is limited to water at sea level and 1 bar of air pressure. Our water would "boil" at 71°C if we were at the summit of Mount Everest, where the pressure is merely 0.34 bar.

Boiling water at room temperature while in a vacuum is a masterful way to illustrate the effect of lowering pressure to lower the boiling temperature of water:

This means that you should consider boiling to be a CHANGE OF STATE from a liquid to a gas, rather than thinking of boiling as equal to 100°C. At -40°C, certain refrigerants can "boil."

One of the most important aspects of the refrigeration cycle process is the interaction between pressure and temperature.

By adjusting its pressure, the refrigerant's condition can be changed from a liquid to a gas.

Refrigerant stays liquid at high pressures; when the pressure is lowered, the liquid refrigerant starts to "boil," turning into a vapour or gas.

With the use of some diagrams, we can go back to the refrigeration cycle and observe how these pressure variations that result in refrigerant state changes truly occur.

Components of the Refrigeration Cycle:

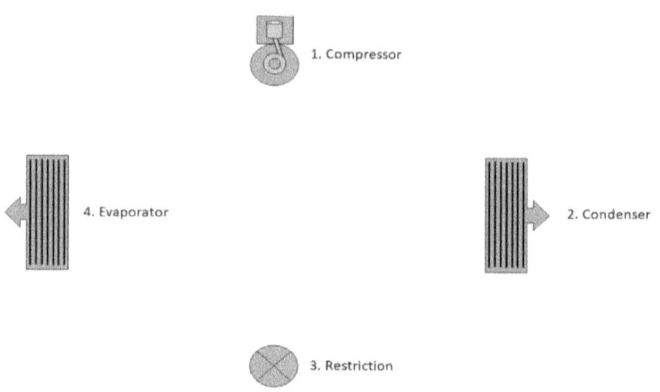

The circuit's four fundamental components are visible here.

The direction of flow in the refrigeration cycle:

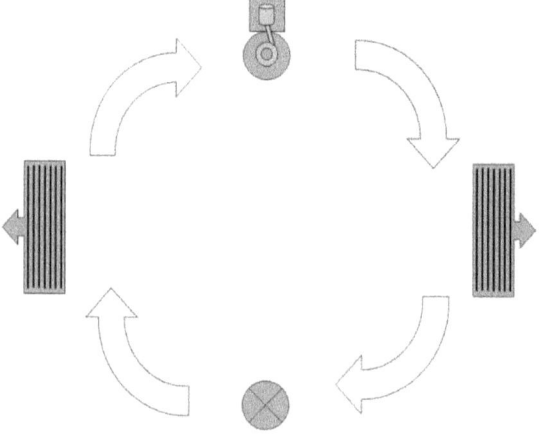

indicates the refrigerant's flow direction, which is clockwise starting at the compressor.

Heat Transfer in the Refrigeration Cycle:

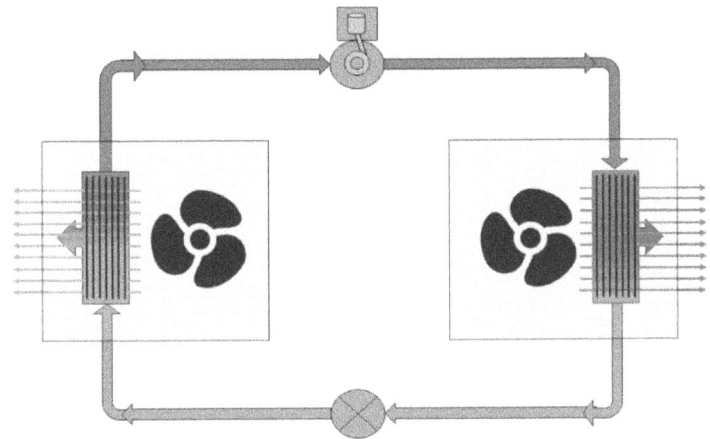

demonstrates the flow of thermal energy. The condenser rejects heat that is absorbed by the evaporator.

The air passing over the evaporator loses heat, making it colder. This colder air is then circulated back into the area being cooled by the evaporator fan.

The condenser, which is often located outside in the open air, rejects the heat that has been removed. It is located outside the area that is being cooled. Over the heated condensing coils, the fan blasts ambient air. This causes the air blasted over the condenser to heat up while cooling and condensing the refrigerant. This explains why hot air is typically blasted at you when you stand in front of a condenser.

Pressures in the Refrigeration Cycle:

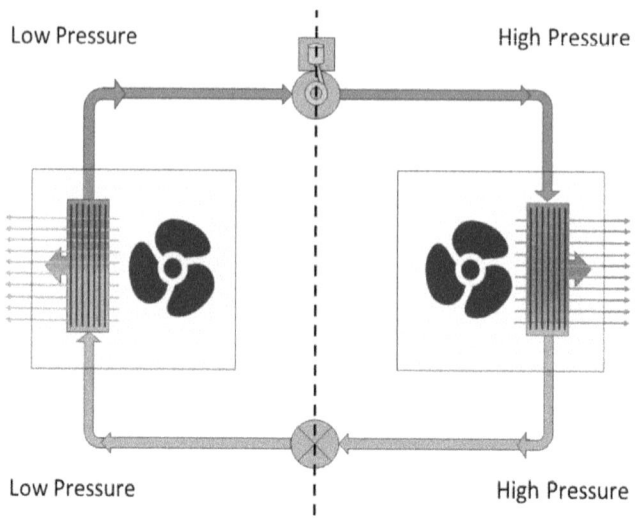

The system can be divided vertically as shown above, showing that the refrigerant is at low pressure at all places to the left of the line and at high pressure at all sites to the right of the line.

The Refrigerant State and the Refrigeration Cycle:

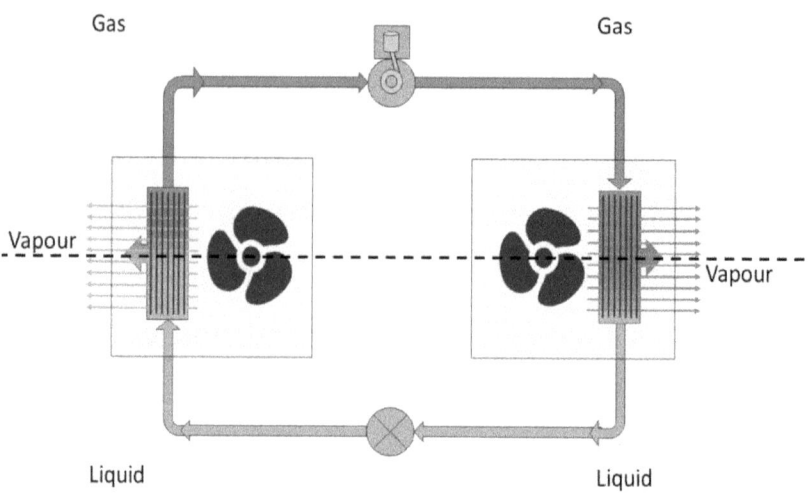

The system can be divided horizontally as shown above to show that the refrigerant is a liquid at all places below the line and a gas at all points above it.

The refrigerant is present in both liquid and gaseous states and is referred to as a vapour in the center of the condenser and evaporator, when the refrigerant changes states.

The Complete Refrigeration Cycle:

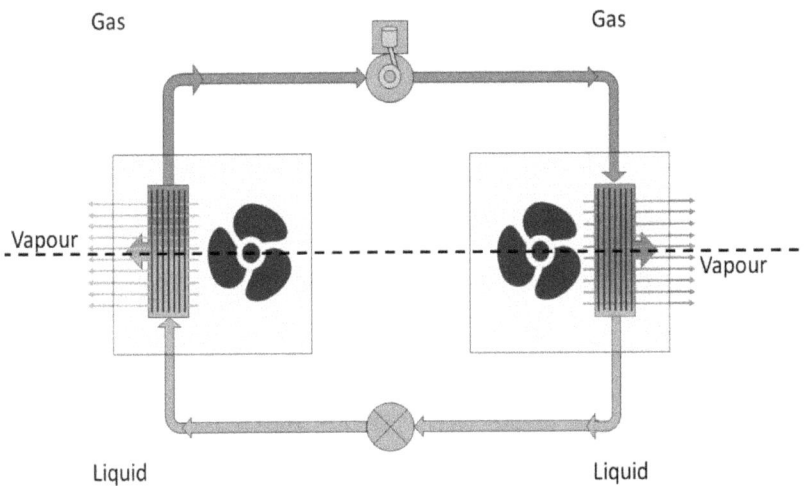

Three new terms have been added to the refrigeration cycle diagram: superheated, saturated, and subcooled.

- **SUPERHEAT:** Heat that is applied to refrigerant vapor beyond and above its boiling point. This guarantees there is no liquid present and the refrigerant is in a gaseous condition.

- **Saturated:** This occurs when there is a mixture of liquid and gas in the refrigerant vapor.
- **Subcooling:** The process of removing heat from refrigerant below its condensing point is known as subcooling. This guarantees that there is no gas present and the refrigerant is in a liquid condition.

In order to guarantee that no liquid returns to the compressor, superheat is crucial. Despite our previous description of the compressor as "acting" like a pump, it is not one. While compressors, as their name implies, compress the volume of the gas to increase both its temperature and pressure, pumps typically transport liquids using an impeller. Liquids cannot be compressed, and if some should return to the compressor, they might seriously harm it.

Because it guarantees that only pure liquid reaches the metering instrument, subcooling is crucial. By doing this, the system's capacity, effectiveness, and dependability are maximized.

Now that we have finished drawing the refrigeration cycle diagram, let's go over the steps in detail:

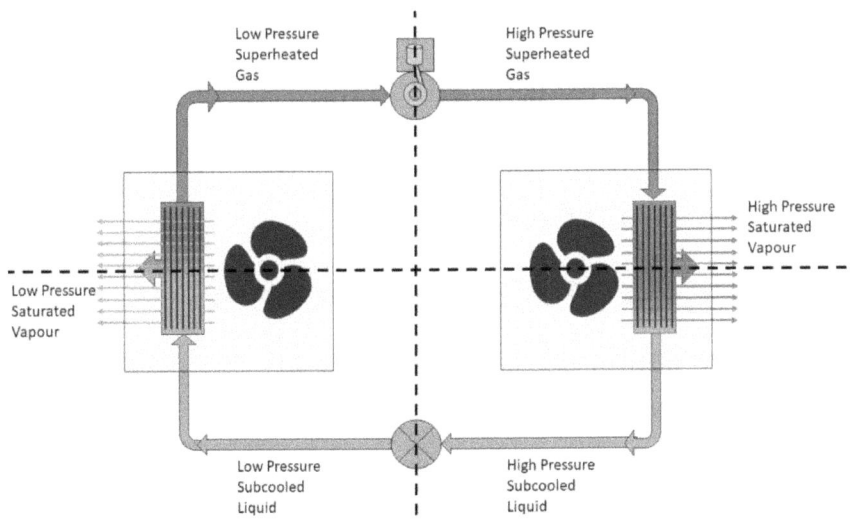

1. Low pressure superheated gas is the state in which the refrigerant enters the compressor.
2. After the gas is compressed by the compressor, it becomes a high pressure superheated gas.
3. The gas inside the condenser starts to cool and transform into a vapour. A high pressure subcooled liquid is formed by the condensation of refrigerant vapour inside the condenser due to further cooling.
4. Recall our earlier example of the nozzle of an aerosol spray can as the high pressure liquid refrigerant flashes off into a vapour as it reaches a low pressure environment through the metering device.
5. Once within the evaporator, the refrigerant vapour absorbs heat from the area being cooled and boils

as a result. The vapour is superheated as it passes through the evaporator coil, converting the refrigerant to gas before it enters the compressor and restarts the cycle.

Types Of Air Conditioners

In actuality, domestic air conditioners are found in more than two thirds of US houses.

There are over ten different kinds of air conditioners available:

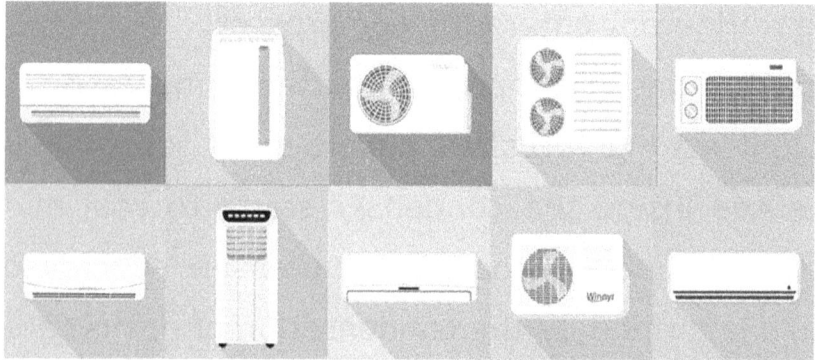

both outside and inside sections of various AC unit kinds.

Selecting a specific AC type is dependent upon:

- **The size of your house** (square footage counts; determine the required capacity using this BTU calculator). For instance, a 1,000 sq. ft. home, a 20,000 BTU portable air conditioner can be used.

For a 3,00 sq. ft. home, a larger 60,000 BTU 5-zone mini-split system will be required.
- Whether you wish to chill one or more rooms or the entire house.
- If you currently have central air installed (**ductwork** is an option).
- Your **spending plan**.

We'll look over every kind of air conditioner with you to determine which one would be most suitable. We'll look at average sizes (measured in BTU), and you'll also obtain a variety of prices for various AC unit kinds.

Consider the energy consumption of each type of air conditioner you are considering for your home, apartment, or space. The smallest 5,000 BTU AC unit can leave you sweating in the heat of summer, while the greatest 60,000 BTU unit will cause your energy bill to soar.

The mini-split air conditioner, the final air conditioner on the list, is quickly rising to the top of the popularity charts.

It is recommended to consistently verify energy-efficiency ratings, such as CEER for window air conditioners, SEER for mini-split units and central air conditioning systems, and EER for portable units.

You want to select the AC unit type that best suits your demands out of all the available options.

Different Kinds of Air Conditioners

Understanding the fundamental workings of an air conditioner is not too difficult.

The first set of metal coils in your system gathers heat from your home, while the second sets it outdoors. The refrigerant, a liquid mixture that transports heat between the two sets of coils, is the crucial component in this situation.

This gives us two sizable categories of air conditioner types:

1. **One standalone air conditioning unit.** Examples include floor-mounted air conditioners, window units, portable air conditioners, and through-the-wall air conditioners.
2. **AC units in a split system (two devices).** Examples include ceiling fans, wall-mounted air conditioners, mini-split air conditioners, and central air conditioners.

Five Types of Stand-Alone Air Conditioning Units

Both coils are contained in a single unit in stand-alone air conditioning units, which are often housed inside.

These AC unit kinds are:

- Easier to transport and install (particularly for portable air conditioners).
- Cheaper to purchase.
- Due to the compressor's interior location, it may be noisier.
- Their capacity is smaller than that of split-system air conditioning units.
- You should always have an air vent outside of a sliding door or window. Somehow, the heated air must escape.

Above all, the stand-alone devices are quite convenient. This kind of air conditioner is the least expensive to purchase and the simplest to install.

These monoblock air conditioners come in five main types:

#1 portable air conditioners (from $200 to $800 in price range)

Most Well-liked, Particularly for Heating Only in One Room

The most common type of air conditioners are portable ones. It's understandable why; portable air conditioners are ideal if you need cooling quickly, affordably, and hassle-free.

They are not required to be installed in or mounted in a certain room. They are as easy to move around as a vacuum cleaner because they are always on wheels and highly mobile.

They are also fairly diminutive. From 5,000 BTU to 14,000 BTU (the largest portable AC units), the capacity is available.

To put things in perspective, an EnergyStar BTU chart indicates that a 10,000 BTU air conditioner, for instance, can adequately chill a 400–450 square foot area.

The disadvantage is that although the AC unit is movable, the air line must also be moved constantly. The house must be evacuated of the heated air. Every portable air conditioner has an air hose (4 to 6 inches in diameter) that can reach up to 10 feet in length for that reason.

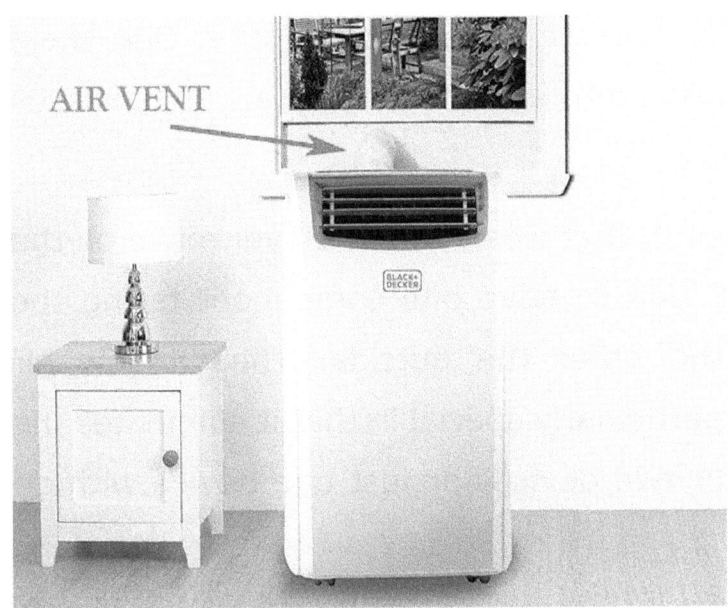

An independent AC unit with an air vent to let out hot air is called a portable air conditioner. It has wheels, so you can easily move it around.

The hose must be attached to the portable air conditioner and the other end must be placed out of a window or sliding door in order to "park" it in a space.

Ultimately, there are a lot of options available to you when selecting the best kind of portable air conditioner. A very decent one may be purchased for less than $500. It's the most adaptable type of air conditioner available.

#2 Window Air Conditioners ($100–$800 in price range)

Europe's "Through-the-Wall" air conditioners

These are fairly popular throughout Europe. One shell, which is integrated into a window or via a wall, encloses the entire unit.

When you about it, that was a rather clever move on the part of the AC unit to have one component facing the interior and the other the outside. The window air conditioner is particularly special in that it eliminates the requirement for two devices or just one device with an air vent.

One side of a window air conditioner faces the interior, and the other side faces the outside. It can be mounted via a wall or a window.

Of course, even with the window air conditioners, things aren't perfect. The wall must be thicker than nine inches if you wish to build it inside of it. When compared to other types of AC units, the window AC unit becomes energy inefficient due to the large walls that typically impede airflow.

The largest window air conditioners have a cooling capacity of up to 25,000 BTU.

In contrast to split-system units, window air conditioners are less expensive and need less installation work. Some more sophisticated types have the added feature of heating as well as cooling. Usually, one with a remote control is also available. Here is the link to the most recent ranking of the top window air conditioners for 2022.

Additionally, the energy-efficient and quietest window air conditioners are available. Among the particular window air conditioners are:

- Vertical air conditioners or cement air conditioners (for narrow windows).
- Window air conditioners with low profiles, which can have up to 80% less profile.

- Saddle over-the-sill window air conditioners: although they rest on the windowsill, the majority of the unit is parallel to the wall and is below the windowsill.

Certain window air conditioners can also function as heat pumps, meaning they can generate heat during the winter. Check out the window AC with heat combos here for more information.

#3 Wall-Mounted Air Conditioning Units (Cost: $300 – $1000)

Ideal for older buildings without a permit for an external unit

A very specialized type of cooling equipment are wall-mounted air conditioners. For those who live in older buildings that get really hot in the summer, these are ideal.

Strong split-system AC units would be ideal for this situation, but most of the older structures are considered to be historic. Consequently, mounting any AC shell on the exterior wall is prohibited.

One option available to you is to wall-mount the AC unit.

These air conditioners can be hung on the wall (the higher, the better) if you have strong supporters. In addition, two air pipes must be installed through the wall behind the AC unit in order for the hot air to be discharged outside. It goes without saying that expert assistance is required for the installation.

Installed against a wall is a wall-mounted air conditioning unit. To get the heated air outside, two pipes pass through the wall.

The air conditioners that are installed through the wall are often larger. Additionally, if you run them at 100%

all the time, the wall behind them may get very hot. If you're not careful, the two air pipes that distribute the heat outside can warm up quite a bit.

While they may cost more, window-mounted air conditioners with built-in heaters can serve as both a summertime cooling source and a winter heating source.

Window AC units typically need an AC support bracket if they are positioned on the outside wall. For instance, installing them is mandated by law in New York City in order to give outside wall units extra stability.

#4 Floor-mounted air conditioners (200–$800 in price range)

Being Replaced by Portable Air Conditioners, Yet Still Usable as Heaters

Wall-mounted air conditioners and floor-mounted air conditioners are fairly comparable. You guessed it: the floor ones' mounting on the floor rather than the wall is pretty much the sole distinction between them.

In order to expel the hot air, this kind of air conditioner furthermore contains two metal pipes that pass through the wall. But we are seeing fewer and fewer of them.

Considering their energy-efficiency, this may be out of the ordinary.

However, unlike portable air conditioners, they are large and bulky, and cannot be stored away during the summer. Although they may be included into older structures, no respectable architect working in the twenty-first century would honestly include them in his designs.

#5 Spot Coolers for Ships and Boats; $1000 – $4000 price range

Large Mobile Industrial AC Units for Specialty Use

These large ones are only for those who own ships, boats, or even airplanes. With a "Spot cooler's" typical capacity of about 30,000 BTU, you can use it to cool a mid-sized yacht.

Large "Spot Cooler" air conditioners are designed to chill entire boats. The hot and cold air exchange is handled by the two pipes.

We bring them up because, in terms of their placement, they are distinct. Spot coolers are movable and situated on the warm side of the boat's outside, or "parked."

The majority of air conditioners are installed on the cold side of the room, inside. Spot coolers consist of two or more pipes that enter the boat and draw in cold air while sucking out warm air.

Split-System Air Conditioning Units (Five Types)

Air conditioners with split systems consist of two shells. The larger, noisier, and more ugly house is outside, whereas the smaller, more attractive one is located within.

This indicates that your home's cooling coil is located inside, while the compressor and heating coil are located outside. These air conditioners come with a number of benefits:

- Since the compressor is outside, they are incredibly quiet.
- They can swiftly and effectively cool your home thanks to their large capacity.
- The interior shell is typically more attractive and smaller.
- Unlike monoblock AC units, there is no requirement for air vents.

The two disadvantages are, of course, that the cost is higher, installation is more difficult, and the outside unit must be attached to your house or somewhere close to it.

Above all, split-system air conditioners are incredibly effective at cooling your entire home.

A few varieties of split-system air conditioners are as follows:

#1 Central Air Conditioners ($4000-$8000 in price range)

An All-Inclusive Fix for Any House (Highest Demand)

Over half of US homes are equipped with "central air." It's a ducted air pipe system, as you are undoubtedly already aware, and it can reach each room in your home or apartment. It is safe to conclude that while central air conditioning is the most difficult to install, it is also the easiest to use.

Typically, this duct-mounted air conditioning system is delivered to your house already installed. The central air conditioner is a terrific option if you're wanting to replace your present AC unit, but the installation process alone might be troublesome. Because you have to break through every ceiling and penetrate every wall, it might cost you up to $10,000.

Central air conditioners, also known as "channel air conditioners," use a combination of outside and internal air to cool the air and give the impression that everything is simple. The central air conditioning unit shell, which is outdoors and typically attached to the house or in the yard, serves as the unit's powerhouse.

The exterior unit that is either in the center of the yard or attached to the house is the main component of a central air conditioner.

It goes without saying that installing the ducked air conditioner piping in your home requires a skilled engineer. You can also get assistance from an air conditioner replacement specialist if you already have a central air conditioning unit. Installing central air just isn't a do-it-yourself task.

Here you can see the prices and brands of the top central air conditioning units.

Wall-mounted and floor-mounted air conditioners (price range: $400 – $3000) are items #2 and #3.

Identical to standalone air conditioners, but with a stronger and quieter split-system installation

There are two types of AC units that can be installed on the wall or the floor: split systems and standalone systems.

Therefore, having a wall-mounted split-system air conditioner with a capacity of 15,000 BTU that is quieter than a portable air conditioner with 6,000 BTU is not rare.

When the floor-mounted air conditioner is installed, it looks like this:

Floor-mounted air conditioner: Two or three internal air conditioners can be installed on one external air shell.

One benefit of this kind of air conditioner is that it may be connected to one outside AC shell (a generator with a ventilator and compressor) to power two or three similar units.

This effectively means that you can have three units—say, 9,000, 12,000, and 15,000 BTU units—within your home. You would have a larger, noisier generator outside the house. The 38,000 BTU capacity of such a system is unattainable for any sort of standalone air conditioner.

#4 Ceiling Type Air Conditioner ($1000 – $10000 Price Range)

Beautiful, High-Capacity Units Ideal for Office Space

The best use for this kind of cassette-style air conditioner is in offices. With its installation on the ceiling, or even suspended from it, the air conditioner is connected to the building's unseen air lines.

The primary benefits of ceiling air conditioners are their power and beauty.

To put it briefly, they typically have a contemporary appearance, don't "jump out" of the wall or the floor, and have an upscale appearance (which, to be honest, they really do). The four outlet louvers are the only elements of the ceiling that "stick out."

The ceiling air conditioner is a powerful and elegant-looking device. ideal for workplaces.

The other component is pure force. One of these cassette air conditioners can replace up to five window air conditioners and up to seven portable air conditioners because the airflow is connected to the central airflow.

The cooling air is moving in a vertical direction rather than a horizontal one due to their position. The majority of wall-mounted air conditioners provide a "sideway breeze." Standing behind the cassette air conditioner will generate a "downward breeze" because it is mounted on the ceiling.

#5: $500–5000 is the price range for mini-split system ductless air conditioners.

The Most Common Large Type Of Air Conditioners Right Now

In the HVAC sector, mini-split air conditioners are gaining popularity. The portable air conditioners with split systems:

- No need for ducting.
- Less expensive to install than central air (you can even find MrCOOL and other DIY mini-splitters).
- Outstanding energy efficiency; as you can see from the top mini-split air conditioners' ranking, their SEER ratings are higher than 20.
- Wide range of capacities: 12,000 to 60,000 BTU.

Understanding the mini-split mechanism is rather simple. One coil is located inside the house or apartment to collect heat within, and the second coil is located outside the building to disperse the heat generated inside.

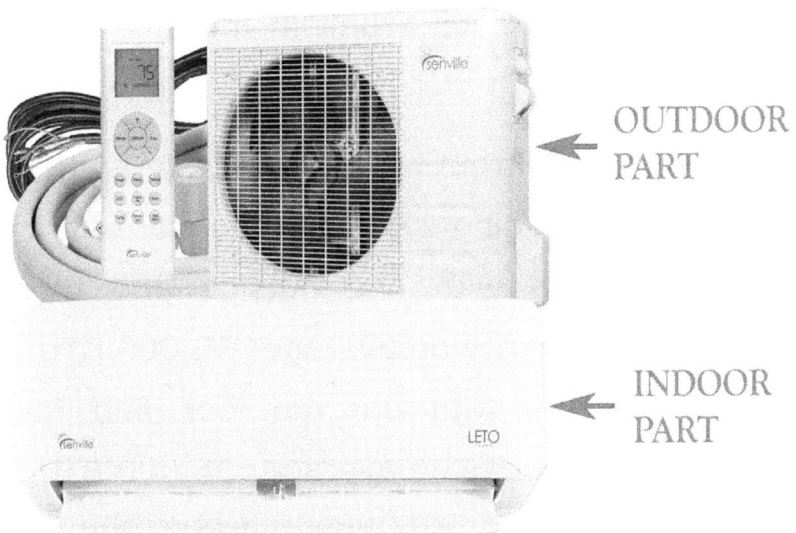

OUTDOOR PART

INDOOR PART

Wall-mounted air conditioner setup: The compressor and ventilator are the unsightly, noisy outside components. The interior is a lovely, peaceful cooling area. With a remote control, adjusting the temperature is simple.

The majority of the time, the floor- or wall-mounted air conditioner's inside shell must be seen and heard. Generally speaking, split-system shells are quieter, more aesthetically pleasing, and smaller.

This is because the AC unit's compressor, which makes the most noise, is housed in the outer shell of the building.

One outdoor and one indoor unit make up the typical mini-split. Systems with the following features are available if you wish to place a unit in multiple rooms with a larger capacity:

- Dual-zone mini-splitters with one outside and two indoor units. Averaging 27,000 BTU of capacity.
- 3-zone mini-splits with one outside and three interior units. Capacity on average: 36,000 BTU.
- 4-zone mini-splits with one outdoor and four interior units. Capacity on average: 36,000 BTU.
- Five-zone mini-splits with one outdoor and five inside units. Capacity average: 48,000 BTU.

Split-system air conditioning machines are typically more powerful but also more expensive and complex.

Select the Type of Air Conditioner Based on Your Requirements

There's no greater guidance for selecting the proper kind of air conditioner than this:

"Select the kind you require."

Some individuals spend $10,000 on a central air conditioning system when a basic portable air conditioner with 6,000 BTUs would be more than adequate.

Some are purchasing a basic portable air conditioner with 6,000 BTUs to cool a 5,000 square foot home in Texas.

Being realistic about the amount of power (BTU) you require is essential to choose the appropriate model of air conditioner for you. Next, determine whether you have an exterior AC shell, are willing to drill holes in your walls, and how quiet you want your air conditioner to be.

Being realistic will always save you a ton of hassle (sweat + money) when a summer heatwave is about to arrive.

What Is A Ductless Air Conditioner?

The terms "ductless," "mini split," and "mounted cooling systems" are probably familiar to you. Describe a ductless air conditioner, please. Yes, that's right—no ductwork. You won't need it if you have a Carrier ductless mini split.

Ductless systems are an effective way to increase your comfort regardless of the challenges your space presents, whether you live in a newer or older home without ductwork, are adding a room addition, converting an existing space, or want more complete year-round climate control over a specific room or area of your home.

A MINI SPLIT AIR COOLER: WHAT IS IT?

How exactly do small split air conditioners operate, and what is its definition? At its most basic, a ductless mini split system consists of an outside unit and an indoor unit connected by electrical cable and refrigerant tubing. Without the need for ducting, the interior unit, which is frequently wall-mounted, provides warm or cooled air directly into the living area. This type of system is known as a single-zone system, and its purpose is to comfortably heat and cool a single area. To offer comfort for the entire house, a Carrier ductless multi-zone system combines one outside unit with up to five internal units.

Ductless HVAC systems are among the simplest and most adaptable to install, as they only require a hole in the wall for the wiring and refrigerant line during installation, and come in a variety of indoor unit styles.

DUCTLESS AIR CONDITIONERS: HOW DO THEY WORK?

Indeed, if we do say so ourselves, pretty darn good. Then, how precisely do ductless air conditioners operate?

The method of cooling used by ductless air conditioners is the same as that of conventional central air conditioning systems. A ductless indoor unit, on the other hand, directs cooled air into a single living room, whereas central air conditioning employs one centrally positioned interior unit that distributes cold air throughout the entire house through a network of ducts and vents.

A full ductless system must have, at the very least, an outside unit with a compressor, condenser coil, and fan, as well as an indoor unit with a blower fan and evaporator coil. Electrical wiring and copper refrigerant tubing link the two units. You can use ductless air conditioning systems in any room of your house:

- High wall units can be installed directly to an interior wall regardless of the height of the room's ceiling.
- Console units function in spaces where wall mounting is either impractical or undesirable.
- If there is room in the ceiling, in-ceiling units are an example of a ducted unit that is concealed from view.
- It is possible to install cassette units straight to the ceiling.
- Based on the square footage of the room, ductless AC units come in a variety of sizes that provide customized heating and cooling.

To reduce noise from patios and outdoor gathering areas into living areas, outdoor units can be positioned strategically. Installation in limited outdoor spaces or on small lots is made possible by narrow cabinets.

Chemical refrigerant is pumped from the outdoor compressor unit to the coil of the indoor unit via the refrigerant pipe. The heat and humidity from the interior air moving across the coil are removed as the liquid refrigerant converts to gas, returning cooler, less humid air to the living area. As heat energy is released through the outdoor coil, the gaseous refrigerant cycles back to the coil and is transformed back into a liquid. With the added capability of heating an interior room in the opposite direction, a ductless heat pump system functions in the exact same manner as a cooling system.

WHAT IS THE ZONE OF A MINI SPLIT AC? System Types: Single and Multi-Zone

When it comes to selecting the ideal ductless air conditioner, what is the zone of a small split air conditioner and what distinguishes single- from multi-zone systems? A single external compressor can power one or more indoor units in a ductless system configuration. Because of their adaptability, ductless systems are great for a variety of spaces, such as sunrooms, garages, and room extensions. They are also a great choice for older homes looking to upgrade their air conditioning.

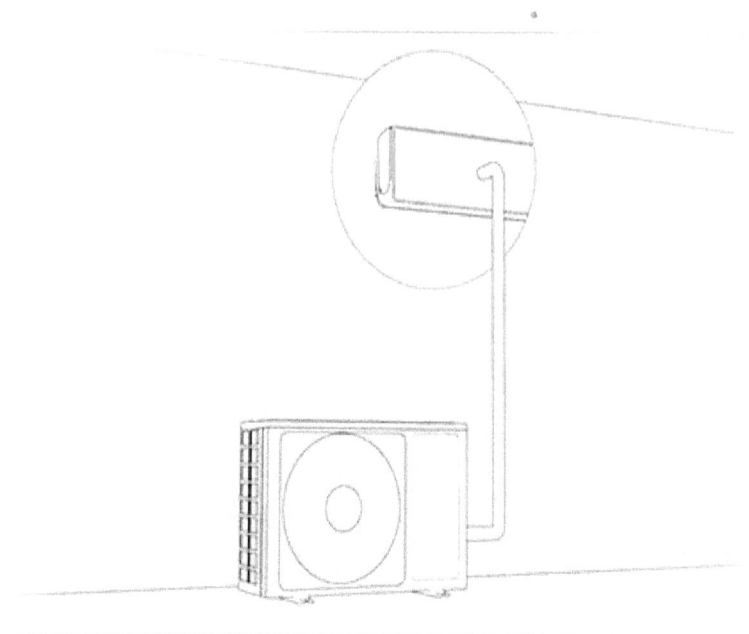

SINGLE- ZONE

It is possible to install ductless heat pumps and air conditioners so that one external compressor and one indoor unit match. A tiny pipe that passes through a tiny aperture and is installed with minimal disruption to your home supplies power and refrigerant to the interior unit from the compressor.

MANY ZONES

Up to five indoor units can be powered by a single outdoor compressor and individually operated by a wireless remote control, giving you a multitude of configuration options for your comfort solutions.

Depending on the maximum number of connectable units, you can even decide to add units to your compressor after installing just two indoor units. This will enable more efficient house remodeling or expansion when funds and time permit.

The Thumper Rules for Ductile Mini Splits

Similar to a Swiss Army knife of HVAC systems are ductless and heat pump systems. They can offer comfort in places where conventional ducted systems are unable to, and they can both cool and heat. extending a house that already exists? Making a living area out of a garage, attic, or basement? giving a room that's constantly too hot or cool a boost?

For all of the aforementioned, there is a solution in a Carrier ductless system. Ductless systems offer an almost infinite number of layouts and a selection of interior units, making them the most flexible and ideal comfort solution. There is no need for ducting, and installation is quick and simple.

You can use ductless systems in addition to your current heat pump or air conditioner. Additionally, they can lower your utility costs by actively heating and cooling only the occupied areas and by using ENERGY STAR qualified systems. By determining the seasonal energy efficiency ratio of a system, you may choose one that will help you use less energy overall. A micro split SEER rating will show you how much energy your system will consume annually. Furthermore, there is no chance of energy loss due to duct leaks. Are we still in the contemplation phase? The benefits and drawbacks of a ductless air conditioner are listed below.

ADVANTAGES OF A DUCTLESS AIR COOLER

- Extremely energy-efficient cooling mechanism
- Simple to install
- No painting, patching, or wiring inside
- Cool a room added to an existing house effectively
- Cool an area that has been transformed into a living area, such as a garage, attic, or basement, effectively
- Maintain the structural integrity of an older house that lacks vents or ductwork space.
- Keep interior décor intact by using low-profile units.
- Boost a room's ability to cool down if it already has air conditioning or has inconsistent temperatures.

DUCTLESS AIR CONDITIONER CONS

- Installing a small split system can cost more than installing a typical ducted system, but in the long run, you might save money on utility bills.
- Mini split units are visible within a room and are wall mounted, in contrast to typical HVAC systems. Nonetheless, the majority of designs are simple and visually pleasing.

WHAT ARE THE BENEFITS OF DUCTLESS AC?

DUCTLESS MINIMAL INSTALLATION

The absence of ducts is one of the numerous advantages of ductless air conditioning! Forget about painting, patching, and hassles when there is no ducting. The installation of your ductless air conditioning system is very inconspicuous and only requires a small hole in the wall to connect the pipe from the inside unit to the outdoor compressor unit. Configuring the system is easy. There is no need for additional interior wiring because the indoor device receives electricity from the outdoor compressor unit.

EFFECTIVE COOLING AND HEATING

No matter the outside weather, Carrier ductless heat pump systems provide year-round comfort management by operating as effective heating and cooling systems even in the most trying circumstances. Certain systems may heat at 80% capacity even at -22°F. In addition, they can cool to 100% capacity in 130°F outside temperatures.

EXACT COOLING AND HEATING

Regardless of where interior units are located, Carrier ductless systems provide precise comfort. Desire a warmer bedroom but a colder home office? Not an issue. One of the numerous advantages of ductless air conditioning is room-based temperature management. Depending on your comfort preferences, rooms might have varying temperatures because units can be regulated independently. Temperature control for heating and cooling is also improved using inverter compressor technology. For your convenience, a variable-speed, inverter-controlled compressor functions similarly to cruise control, replacing the frequent up-and-down temperature fluctuations provided by standard single-stage systems. It effectively regulates interior temperature fluctuations to a minimum.

SILENT PERFORMANCE

Never undervalue how important silent operation is to your general well-being. Because of this, the best air conditioning and heating systems should be acknowledged rather than ignored. The comfort cycles of Carrier ductless outdoor units with inverter-controlled variable-speed compressors are quieter, slower, and longer-lasting. It is also possible to install the outdoor unit farther away from patios, decks, and other outdoor living areas thanks to long refrigerant lines.

ALLERGY MANAGEMENT

Ductless micro split systems produce cleaner air in the rooms where they are installed since each indoor unit has filters. regulating air quality is equally as important as regulating air temperature when using ductless heating and cooling. There is no air cross-contamination between rooms when circulation is controlled inside a small area.

COMMON QUESTIONS CONCERNING DUCTLESS MINI SPLITS

DO DUCTLESS AIR CONDITIONS USE OUTSIDE AIR TO PULL IN AIR?

No, air from outside your space is not drawn in by ductless air conditioners. Similar to an HVAC ducted system, ductless systems recycle the air already present in your house.

DO YOU NEED TO VENT DUCTLESS AC?

Not at all! Since a ductless AC system doesn't produce any hazardous gases, your house doesn't need to be vented.

IS THE AIR PURIFIED BY A DUCTLESS AC?

Indeed, as ductless indoor units come with an air filter, they can aid in air purification. By capturing undesirable particles, the air filter helps keep them from returning to your house.

ARE MINI SPLITS A CARBON MONOXIDE PRODUCER?

No, carbon monoxide cannot be produced by a small split system.

The advantages of ductless air conditioning are abundant. Speak with a local Carrier ductless expert to determine whether a ductless air conditioner is a good fit for your house and to receive an estimate.

WHAT MAKES A MINI SPLIT DIFFERENT FROM AN AIR CONDITIONER?

The method by which a central air conditioner and a small split system introduce cool air into your house differs significantly.

A system of ducts is used by an air conditioner to provide cool air throughout your house. Cool air is provided by registers or vents, and the ducts are usually put in the walls, ceilings, or floors. Warm air is distributed through the same ductwork used to install central air conditioners as part of forced-air heating systems. This occurs during the heating season. A mini-split system, on the other hand, distributes cool air without the need of ducts. Instead, each room or zone in your house has one or more indoor units fixed on the wall or ceiling. The conduit that holds the power cable, refrigerant tubing, and condensate drain connects these inside units to an outdoor unit. Every indoor unit has a thermostat, enabling precise temperature control in every space.

A mini split is generally more energy-efficient than an air conditioner, which is another distinction between the two. Cool air can be delivered directly to the room where it is needed using a micro split system, eliminating the potential for energy loss caused by ducting. Furthermore, inverter-driven compressors, which are commonly found in mini splits, may modify the cooling output to correspond with the requirements of each rooms, therefore reducing energy waste.

All things considered, the choice between a mini split and a central air conditioner depends on a number of variables, such as your budget, your home's size, and your cooling requirements. A central air conditioner might be a more sensible option if your house is larger or if you need to cool more than one room or zone. However, since it may be highly expensive to install ductwork in an existing home, a micro split system might be a smart choice if your house is already without ducting. Additionally, a ductless system can be a better choice if you desire energy efficiency and customized temperature control.

A MINI SPLIT SYSTEM: WHAT IS IT?

The phrases mini-split and mini-split system are synonymous and can be used interchangeably.

An outside unit plus one or more indoor units make up a mini-split, sometimes referred to as a ductless mini-split system, which is a kind of heating and cooling system.

Usually wall-mounted, the interior units are linked to the outdoor unit through a tiny tube that also holds the condensate drain, power cable, and refrigerant tubing. Every indoor unit has a thermostat, enabling precise temperature control in every space.

A mini-split system's primary benefit is its adaptability in offering zonal heating and cooling. You may select which spaces or rooms to chill using a mini-split system, and you can change the temperature in each zone separately. This implies that instead of cooling your entire house, you can conserve energy by just cooling the rooms you use.

Because mini-split systems don't require ductwork, which can be a source of energy loss, they are also simple to install. Furthermore, because they can eliminate the energy losses connected with ductwork, mini-split air conditioning systems are frequently more energy-efficient than central air conditioning systems.

Chapter 6

What are HVAC controls and how do they work?

By 2023, the HVAC controls market is expected to have grown from USD 13.6 billion in 2018 to USD 27.0 billion, so it's definitely something you should be watching. We'll try our best to assist you in taking the initial step toward learning more about these systems and how they operate, whether you are new to the HVAC sector or you just want to know more about building operations or energy usage.

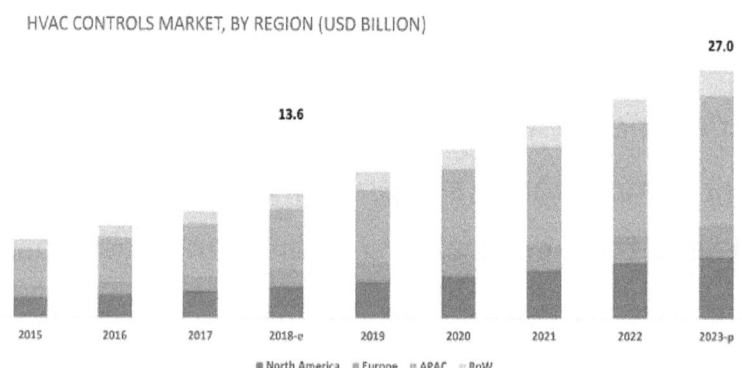

How do HVAC controls work?

The term "HVAC control systems" can refer to a variety of applications, from simple home settings to potentially highly intricate commercial settings. In general, however, HVAC controls are made up of devices that regulate the functioning of HVAC (heating, ventilation, and air conditioning) equipment.

In most homes, a thermostat is wired to a self-contained air conditioning unit of some sort. You are managing the operations of that standalone device by modifying the temperature (or setpoint). For instance:

Setting your summer thermostat to 75 degrees means that your air conditioning unit will have to run until the temperature inside your home hits 75 degrees, at which time it will have to turn off.

Because it senses the temperature within your home, your thermostat functions as both a sensor and an HVAC controller in this straightforward example. As we get deeper into more intricate systems, we'll talk more about sensors.

When it comes to implementing HVAC control systems in larger establishments, the controls themselves are occasionally a component of a more comprehensive system called an energy management system or building automation system.

Systems for Building Automation

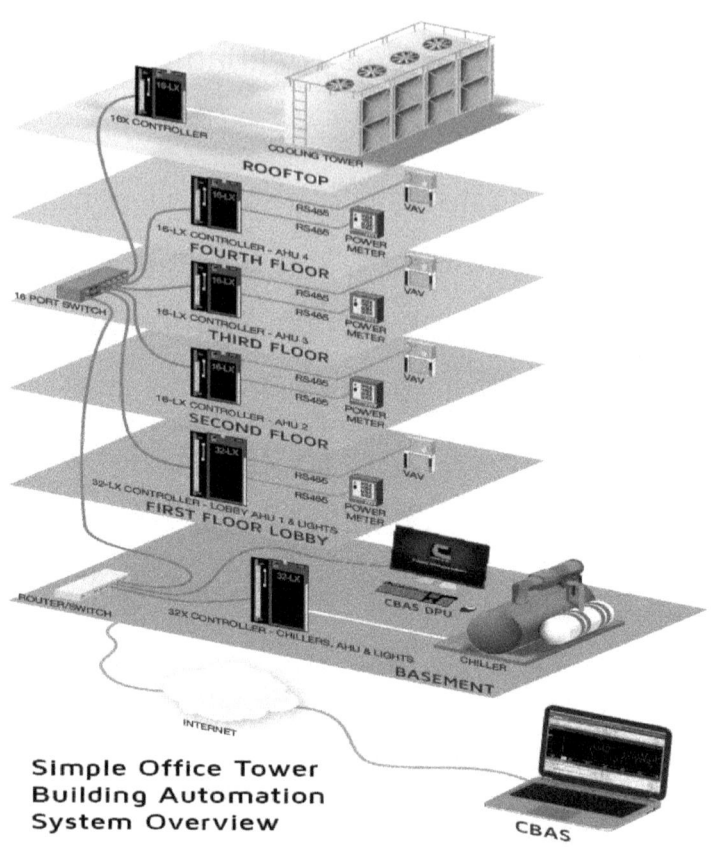

Simple Office Tower
Building Automation
System Overview

Large buildings frequently have highly complicated mechanical systems that must operate effectively to be both effective and energy-efficient. The equipment for HVAC, lighting, fire alarm, and access/security systems is often managed by building automation systems, or BAS.

When trying to construct sequences of processes to make a building "smart," it can be helpful to have these consolidated under one software platform; nevertheless, some building operators see this as a risk having "all their eggs in one basket." Our attention will remain on independent HVAC control systems.

To make things easier, we will divide the standard BAS into four main categories:

1. Head-end hardware and software
2. Network Configuration
3. Supervisors
4. Final Products

As your knowledge of HVAC controls grows, you'll discover that many pieces of equipment fall into more than one of these categories; still, we'll try to provide straightforward examples for each.

Head-end computer/Software

There are several names for the head-end computer/software, including front-end, workstation, and energy management software. An operator can view field operations through this central user interface and deliver control functions as needed. By keeping an eye on the system inputs, users may view the outcomes of the control signals that are provided. The zone temperature would decrease, for instance, if an air duct damper that was previously closed was ordered to open.

Network Infrastructure

The network infrastructure of a contemporary HVAC controls system normally consists of RS-485 twisted pair wires and CAT-5/6 Ethernet. The RS-485 wires handle communication between the controllers and field devices, while the CAT 5/6 Ethernet connection typically transports messages from the head-end to and from the controllers.

Controllers

a device that offers a way to monitor and/or control end devices and is connected to the network infrastructure.

Final Products

These gadgets include actuators that transform energy into mechanical force, relay switches that open and close circuits, and sensors that gauge the value of variables like temperature or humidity. There are many different endpoints. These are only a handful.

These four parts work together to form an HVAC controls system, which has as its main objective ensuring occupant safety and comfort while maximizing energy efficiency.

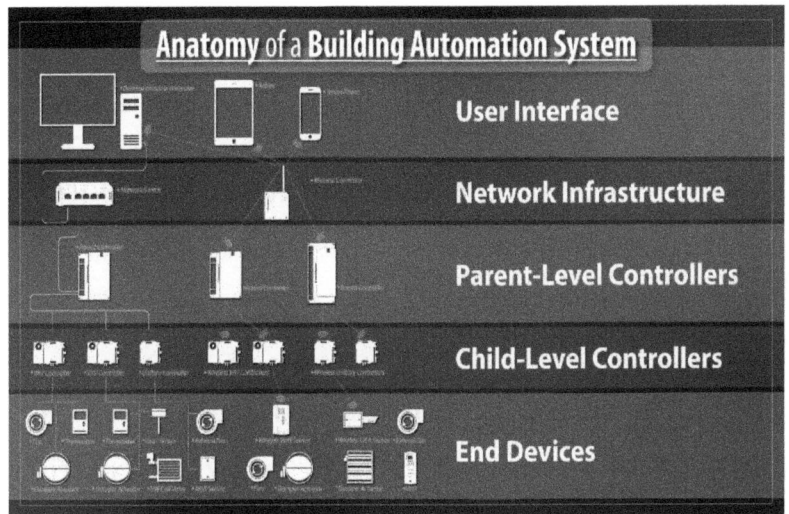

How do controls for HVAC systems operate?

It is necessary to first comprehend what a sequence of activities is in order to comprehend how HVAC control systems operate. HVAC systems are automated by a series of steps, commonly referred to as a logic statement, that are triggered by simultaneous activities of other pieces of equipment and sensor input data.

Let's take another straightforward example where you have an office in a business building and you have your side of the office's thermostat set to 75 degrees. The thermostat sends this input back to a controller via network infrastructure, which then uses the feedback to carry out the next steps.

When the temperature inside the building rises above 75 degrees,

Start the A/C unit after that.

When the temperature of the interior air is 75 degrees or lower,

After that, turn off the A/C.

We may fine-tune those sequences to guarantee the best possible comfort and energy efficiency by crafting statements that tell the equipment how to operate under specific circumstances. Additionally, it saves us from having to manually switch on and off equipment.

Larger HVAC systems and more sophisticated equipment, as you might expect, correspond to larger and more intricate operating sequences. A number of priority levels will also be present in these larger systems, allowing you to choose which orders an equipment piece should be obeying. To keep things simple, let's assume there are three priority levels:

1. Handler

2. How to Program Logic
3. Weekly Timetable

Operator: This denotes that the person operating the system is giving direct instructions on how it should function.

Logic programming: This refers to the execution of the machinery according to the previously discussed order of operations.

The weekly schedule indicates which days and hours the equipment should be turned on and off.

The Weekly Schedule has the lowest priority in this case, whereas Operator has the highest, indicating that Operator takes precedence over the other two. In this example, we will cool a floor using an air handling unit (AHU) that runs early in the morning.

The AHU's controller will initially check to verify if the operator is giving it commands. The building engineer would only need to use the Operator command if they noticed anomalies that warranted turning on the AHU earlier than usual or possibly not using it at all.

The AHU controller will then check the Logic Programming, which states that the AHU must activate if the interior air temperature is more than 80 degrees at six in the morning. This sequence is designed to kick in early on exceptionally warm mornings, allowing the AHU to get a head start if necessary.

If this isn't the case, the AHU controller will check the Weekly Schedule to see what instructions it contains. The air handler will operate Monday through Friday from 7 a.m. to 5 p.m., according to the weekly schedule.

Hopefully, this example captures the essence of how priority levels function, however there are many layers of logic and a few more priority levels in real-life applications.

HVAC Control Types

A facility is most likely outfitted with a contemporary controls system called Direct Digital Controls (DDC) if it was built or renovated within the last ten to twenty years. Similar to the majority of modern technology, these systems exchange signals using electrical means.

Pneumatic HVAC controls are sometimes found in older buildings. These control circuits use mechanical ways to accomplish control functions and are based on air pressure. While more modern pneumatic systems are occasionally available, DDC offers several advantages.

HVAC Control System Advantages

Ensuring occupant comfort in buildings is the main objective and advantage of HVAC controls. A DDC system's precision control combined with the input data allows you to almost completely remove hot and cold spots in a building.

Nearly half of the energy used in a commercial building is typically used for HVAC operations. Facility managers can drastically cut their energy expenses and environmental impact by implementing management systems that minimize energy consumption.

You may automate your HVAC system's operations with a correctly operating HVAC controls system, freeing up your time to handle other urgent tasks. As Ben Franklin once remarked, "Time is money."

Safety is another important benefit that these technologies offer that was previously underappreciated. As we work to provide a healthy atmosphere for every building tenant, having control over a facility's air quality is more crucial than ever.

Thermostats

Smart thermostats automatically respond to your behavior and the changing weather, saving you money, energy, and time.

The cost of heating and cooling your house accounts for about half of your energy expenditure. For even higher energy savings, smart thermostats combine automation and sensors. With a smartphone, they may also be remotely monitored and controlled. In contrast, programmable thermostats conserve energy as well, but they don't react to changes in the weather or the presence of people. Furthermore, manual thermostats need to be adjusted immediately. A smart thermostat is the most convenient to use out of the three.

Smart Thermostats

The average programmable thermostat is far less expensive than a smart thermostat. However, it's a good option if it fits inside your budget and you have wireless internet—rebate opportunities are now available. Over time, smart thermostats learn from your consumption, record any changes you make, and even detect whether a room is occupied. Most importantly, they give you unmatched control over heating and cooling, which lowers usage and saves money. Having a smart thermostat system installed by a professional is recommended.

- Suitable with the majority of central heating systems

- Remote control and ease of use are benefits for residents
- A lot of them can link to real-time weather data, allowing them to make adjustments instantly.

Thermostats: Mechanical and Programmable

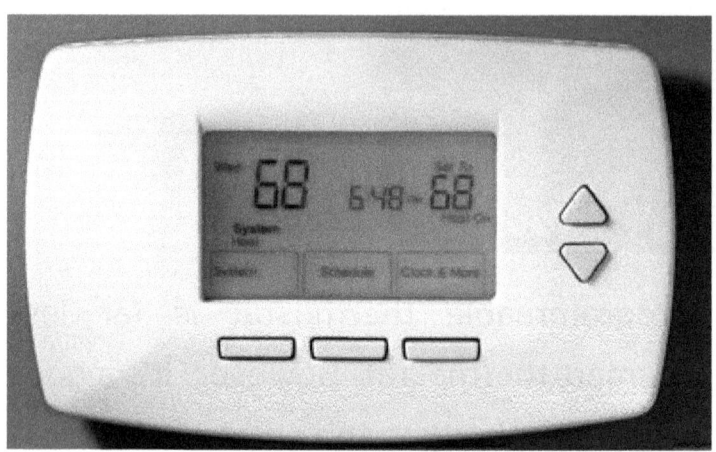

Analog thermostats with a dial design have been around since the middle of the 20th century. They remain fairly accurate when adjusted appropriately. They must be kept out of the path of drafts, sunshine, and heat and cold sources, just like any other thermostat. Digital programmable models provide with energy-saving features like vacation override and let you set temperatures ahead of time. If you're not ready for a smart thermostat, they're a good compromise.

Programmable Thermostat Advantages

Nationwide, programmable thermostats are starting to become commonplace in households. Many are discovering that switching to a programmable thermostat alone helps their pocketbook.

Programmable thermostats are not only an excellent smart home appliance but also offer several benefits to air conditioning systems. Since these thermostats are now the norm in most places, you and your staff should be marketing them as an HVAC company.

Let's examine some of these client perks as well as the many kinds of choices that are offered.

Advantages of Programmable Thermostats

Saves Cash

Cost savings are arguably the biggest advantage of a programmable thermostat and the primary factor in the migration of many users to one.

The greatest strategy to deal with growing energy expenses is to use less energy. Customers can use programmable thermostats to control the climate while they are away or change the temperature to suit their comfort levels.

For each degree that the thermostat is adjusted, homeowners can save roughly 2% of their energy expenditure, depending on the season. You can also make a timetable that you adhere to when you're not at home.

For your customers, the most compelling aspect could be the cost reduction. Use concrete cost reductions in your sales presentations, if at all possible.

Steady Temperature

The ability of programmable thermostats to keep the house at a constant temperature is a major benefit.

Programmable thermostats allow the air conditioner to run at a steady temperature during the warmer months, and the opposite is true during the colder months. Significant hot or cold patches in various parts of the house are avoided as a result.

Higher Level Features

Advanced functions are frequently included with programmable thermostats. Customers may be able to adjust the temperature of their houses from a distance, depending on the thermostat.

Certain thermostats come equipped with features like Bluetooth, Google or Alexa compatibility, Wi-Fi connectivity, smartphone syncing, and even the ability to integrate with your local weather forecast. Before assisting your customer in selecting the greatest features, be sure to talk about their specific wants.

Heating and cooling zones

A programmable thermostat can assist in controlling the temperature in each of a home's climate zones. You may personalize every space in a house with controls located in each zone.

Enhances HVAC Units

A customer's system will function more effectively if they pair their HVAC system with a programmable thermostat.

By installing a programmable thermostat, you can extend the life of an older HVAC system for a customer that might be approaching its end of its useful life. By doing so, the system will be able to function at peak efficiency and experience less strain.

Reduces Time

Customers can spend less time changing the temperature when using programmable thermostats.

Customers using manual thermostats must adjust the temperature at various times of the day. Customers need to make more adjustments before they depart when it's time to leave. It gets really tiresome after a time.

Nevertheless, all of those problems can be solved with a programmable thermostat. Customers may forget about a thermostat after it is set and carry on with their day, confident that it is functioning properly.

Different Types of Programmable Thermostats

There are other types of programmable thermostats than smart thermostats, as you may already be aware. The most common varieties of programmable thermostats are as follows:

1. 7-Day Thermostats: This kind of programmable thermostat is ideal for houses where the temperature is adjusted on a daily basis. Families or people with busy schedules, for instance, would

find this style useful. Furthermore, it is the most adaptable kind of programmable thermostat.

2. 5+2 Thermostats: Designed for people who usually work a five-day workweek and take a two-day weekend. In essence, it suits people who prefer to have one workweek routine and a separate weekend plan.

3. 5+1+1 Thermostats: These enable users to schedule both weekends and workdays.

4. Smart Thermostat: Wi-Fi enabled and programmable from a computer or smartphone, smart thermostats are the most popular kind of programmable thermostat. For people who have erratic schedules or who might forget to adjust their thermostat, this kind works nicely. An app is typically included with smart thermostats to facilitate simple programming when the user is away from home. They also let the homeowner monitor the energy they save.

5. The learning smart thermostat is one that automatically sets up a schedule based on its observations of your household's daily routine. They are Wi-Fi enabled and can be remotely programmed via a computer or smartphone, just

like smart thermostats. This is a fantastic alternative for people who have a regular schedule and don't want to bother setting it themselves.
6. Thermostats designed expressly for use with heat-pump systems are known as heat-pump specific thermostats. When used in conjunction with heat pump systems, energy consumption can outweigh the energy-saving advantages of programmable thermostats.

Once more, while recommending a programmable thermostat to a customer, make sure to address their particular needs. While some consumers might prefer a more hands-off approach, others would like to have complete control over their smart thermostat.

How Zoning Can Improve Your HVAC Energy Efficiency

Comfort and energy efficiency should be your top concerns when it comes to heating and cooling your house. Both of these advantages can be obtained by installing a zoning system in your forced air HVAC system.

Installing ventilation duct dampers and a central control panel with several thermostats are required for the zoning system in order to regulate each zone in your home. When it comes to installing zoning systems in the Cuyahoga Falls, OH area, Keith Heating & Cooling is the company to contact.

Here's how zoning systems can enhance both the comfort of your house and the energy efficiency of your HVAC system.

Zoning systems independently heat and cool each room.

Although zoning HVAC systems are quite sophisticated, they essentially divide your home into several temperature zones that may be independently managed.

Even if the product and concept are straightforward, a professional will still need to evaluate your existing system configuration, your comfort issues, and your comfort preferences in order to develop the zoning system that will maximize both comfort and energy economy.

Separate temperature control is made possible throughout the house via zoning.

A zoning system can address the issue if certain rooms or sections of your house don't receive comfortable temperatures like the rest of the house. You'll be able to direct additional heated or cooled air solely to the spaces or rooms that require it.

Let's take an example where your property faces west and receives the most sunlight during the hottest part of the day, meaning that your front rooms stay warmer during the summer. You can cool those rooms with a zoning system instead of requiring the air conditioner to maintain the same cool temperature in the other rooms.

Energy savings equal to less strain on your HVAC system.

The majority of individuals shut off the air vents in a room they don't use or in a section of their home that is excessively hot or cold relative to the rest of the house. Your HVAC system experiences strain when the vent ducts are closed, which reduces airflow and air pressure and shortens the life of your heat pump or air conditioner.

Your HVAC system won't have to work as hard to heat or cool the more challenging regions of your home when you can individually adjust the temperature in each room or section of the house. The ventilation system's dampers are positioned such that they do not create a backflow issue.

You won't need to shut off the ventilation ducts since the central control system will adjust the dampers as needed.

More Coziness With Less Power

Every family in Cuyahoga Falls values comfort highly, yet a lot of them forgo comfort in order to save the energy expenditures associated with heating and cooling their homes. Installing a zoning system allows you to take advantage of the energy savings that come with having the ability to adjust the temperature in each room or zone to your preference.

Chapter 7

Guide to HVAC Energy Efficiency

What Is HVAC Energy Efficiency?

Operating your HVAC system and related equipment as efficiently as feasible without sacrificing temperature, humidity, differential pressure, zone ventilation needs, etc. will result in HVAC energy efficiency. Merely curbing energy usage is useless if it affects how the facility operates.

Why Is HVAC Systems' Energy Efficiency Important?

Generally speaking, HVAC systems are among the biggest energy users in a building, especially when boilers and chillers are included. HVAC should therefore be the main focus of any efforts made by a facility in order to significantly effect their energy, cost, and carbon emission reduction aims.

What Advantages Do Effective HVAC Systems Offer?

There are several advantages to increasing HVAC system efficiency, some of them are as follows:

- Lower expenses
- Lower carbon emissions, which can help achieve net-zero goals
- Better zone conditions, including ventilation, temperature regulation, and compliance;
- greater equipment life cycle, minimizing excessive operation;
- Lower downtime of equipment, leading to greater production uptime;
- Higher occupant satisfaction, resulting in fewer complaints from employees or tenants

The Best Upgrades for HVAC Energy Efficiency

Make Sure Proper Maintenance Procedures

Improving HVAC energy efficiency and performance starts with making sure that systems are properly maintained. To maintain optimal operation, equipment including boilers, chillers, and air handling units (AHUs) has to have routine maintenance inspections.

The following are some crucial equipment maintenance tasks that will affect energy efficiency:

Air Handling Units (AHUs):

- Clean water coils
- Verify that there are no air leaks from panels and water leaks from coils and pipes
- Verify that damper linkages are secure and dampers are not leaking
- Verify calibration of important control sensors (temperature, humidity, differential pressure, etc.)

Boilers:

- Verify that the temperature and differential pressure control sensors are calibrated;
- Check for leaks in the system;
- Verify that the water levels are sufficient;
- Verify that the boiler insulation is fitted appropriately.

Chillers:

- Verify that the temperature and differential pressure control sensors are calibrated;
- Make sure the strainers are clean;
- Clean the tubes and filters in the chillers;
- Verify that the oil levels are proper.

Diminish A Superfluous Operation

Excessive operation is often the cause of excessive energy consumption in HVAC equipment. This can happen via mismanaged time schedules or, more frequently, from turning off automatic equipment.

This may occur if the HVAC equipment is physically overridden at the equipment or at the BMS, but not switched back to automated mode. Such a scenario usually arises when maintenance is performed on the machinery or when an operator temporarily overrides a piece of equipment to run or stop in order to satisfy a field requirement.

Eliminate Inherent Control Points

Many of the commissioned set points and parameters are frequently overridden at the building management system (BMS) over time. According to this, either:

A. The machinery can be operating too aggressively to reach unnecessary set points.

B. Inadequate control algorithms are not meeting zone requirements effectively.

To make sure that override points are kept to a minimum and taken into consideration, BMS system set points and parameters should be regularly evaluated. On the BMS, overridden points should never be a long-term fix.

Make sure the actual installation is appropriate.

HVAC efficiency is reduced if the installation is insufficient for the intended use. A temperature sensor placed adjacent to a vending machine could be the physical installation that causes the AHU to overcool the zone. Another possibility is that a badly placed sensor in a duct is misinterpreting the temperature of the return air, preventing you from taking full advantage of the free cooling capacity.

When zones are repurposed for other purposes and the AHUs can no longer function effectively because of capacity or design difficulties, this is another common problem.

For instance, controlling humidity currently requires a zone with equipment solely intended for heating and cooling, but the cooling coil is not large enough to sufficiently dehumidify the air.

Verify that control algorithms are appropriate for the application and functioning as intended.

The key to guaranteeing the energy-efficient operation of your HVAC plant and equipment is having control algorithms that are properly calibrated and functioning. HVAC consumption can be lowered by up to 30% by making sure the control loops are functioning properly.

Your BMS has several important control loops that determine how your system functions. For this reason, it is crucial to develop, commission, and monitor these control algorithms. A few to check out are:

- Air handling units (AHUs):
- economy mode (free cooling);
- supply air pressure control and pressure reset;
- supply air temperature control and temperature reset;
- VAV controls

Chillers:

- Control and reset of chilled water temperature;
- Control of primary and secondary pumps;
- Reset of condenser water temperature;
- Chiller staging parameters

Boilers

- pump controls

- boiler staging parameters
- boiler temperature control, and temperature reset

How Can Energy Costs Be Cut Using HVAC Analytics Software?

Help In The Maintenance

Having building analytics software keep an eye on your machinery and plants might assist identify areas that need more maintenance attention. This entails switching from preventative to data-driven maintenance, which will decrease complaints and increase productivity and resource efficiency. It will also assist reduce downtime.

Many parts, including valves, dampers, and sensors, won't need to be physically checked as often if the equipment is continuously monitored.

Monitor Excessive Function

Building analytics solutions discover how buildings should function by tracking and evaluating the data. The system will sound an alert for examination if equipment starts to quickly deviate, identifying the locations of any abrupt changes to working hours or specifications. This guarantees prompt issue resolution.

Make Sure Everything Is Installed Properly

Building analytics platforms monitor and analyze the numerous control parameters to determine when equipment is not working efficiently.

There are several reasons why equipment may not be functioning effectively or meeting the necessary conditions, and in certain cases, inadequate installation or design may be the cause.

The building analytics platform can offer advice on the problem and possible fixes, including any installation-related problems, based on the control anomalies. This simplifies the correction.

Verify that Control Algorithms Are Appropriate for the Application and Function Correctly.

The location and timing of the absence of optimal control algorithms can be determined by building analytics platforms. By analyzing operational inefficiencies inside systems and subsystems, the analytics platform can make sure that relationships are functioning well.

Examining, for instance, the effects of VAV operation on AHU operation, which in turn affects the operation of the boiler and chiller, is one way to achieve this. Any modifications made to one system that affects another will be noted and reported as a matter for further research.

Control logic inefficiencies can sometimes go unreported for years since the space conditions are not affected by the badly performing control loops, which makes them difficult to diagnose without the right tools or understanding. The system may not be performing at its best even when the requirements are being met.

Why Is HVAC Maintenance Important?

For many homeowners, HVAC systems can be expensive but important investments. You wouldn't use your HVAC system without performing routine HVAC maintenance, just as you wouldn't drive a car without ever changing the oil.

Maintaining your HVAC system properly will increase its lifespan, prevent expensive repairs from needing to be made, and guarantee that it is running at peak efficiency.

1. way to reduce energy consumption

The efficiency of your HVAC system will be maintained when you work with a reputable professional. The numerous components of your HVAC system will be carefully tested, inspected, and cleaned as part of preventative maintenance. By taking this action, you can ensure that the system is operating as efficiently as possible.

Your HVAC system won't have to work as hard to provide comfort for you and your family when it's operating as effectively as possible. As a result, your energy consumption will decrease and your electricity bill will decrease.

If you don't maintain your HVAC system, it will eventually have to work harder and harder to achieve the same output. For instance, your filters will clog with dust and debris if you don't clean and replace them. This will significantly reduce circulation and make your air conditioner and heater work harder to cool or heat your house. Additionally, it may result in parts wearing out earlier than they otherwise would.

2. Avoiding Expensive Repairs

When you perform preventative maintenance, you can avoid having to hire an emergency AC repair service. On a preventative maintenance service call, a qualified HVAC expert will be able to identify trouble spots. This will enable you to address any problems before they become more significant.

Early detection allows for the repair of numerous defects as well as normal wear and tear. Additionally, they are less stressful and more affordably fixed. Temperate weather in the fall and spring allows for the maintenance of HVAC systems, so any repairs will not be as bothersome as they would be in the thick of the summer or winter.

Small problems with your HVAC system can easily grow into much greater, more significant problems if you don't obtain regular maintenance for it. There may be a line if the weather is really bad because there is typically a significant demand for HVAC service calls during these times.

You will be forced to endure the summer's heat or the winter's cold while the replacement or repair is being done if you have an HVAC emergency. You'll significantly lower your likelihood of encountering emergencies by practicing good maintenance.

3. Compliance with Warranty Conditions

If the HVAC components are still covered by warranty, be aware that many manufacturers will not honor a claim unless they have proof of yearly maintenance. In essence, you're purchasing insurance when you pay for routine HVAC repair.

If you have proof of maintenance, your HVAC technician will be able to file a claim with greater ease and confidence if something goes wrong and it's covered under your warranty. To make things easier for customers, if you continue to work with the same HVAC firm, they might have all of these maintenance documents and equipment warranties on file.

An annual maintenance record for your HVAC system will help you sell your house more quickly. Which house would you select if you could choose between ones where the HVAC system has received regular maintenance and ones where it hasn't? We decide on the house with the well-maintained HVAC system. Extra credit is awarded for possessing every record.

4. Enhancement of Your Home's Air Quality

The air quality in your house or place of business will be improved if your HVAC system is operating at peak performance. Your HVAC system's function includes removing impurities from the air that you, your family, and your coworkers breathe.

Ninety percent of Americans' time is spent indoors. The Environmental Protection Agency (EPA) reports that, shockingly, indoor concentrations of several contaminants are two to five times greater than average outside values.

You won't be able to filter out many of these dangerous particles that can cause headaches, asthma attacks, and inflammation of the lungs if you neglect your HVAC system.

If you do not clean or use a UV lamp on your indoor evaporator coil, bacteria and mold might grow there because it is a wet and humid environment. More allergy problems for everyone in your house or place of business as a result.

The ability of a clean filter to capture airborne particles and prevent air contamination will be improved. (Change an interior air filter yourself is also quite simple!) Your house will be healthier with a clean heat pump or air conditioner coil. An in-duct or whole-house air purification system can actively filter the air to an even higher quality while maintaining the cleanliness of your system.

5. HVAC Maintenance and Health and Safety

Regular HVAC maintenance will help you and your family stay safer in your house. This is so that your HVAC specialist can check for any carbon monoxide leaks, which might be lethal to anybody within the house. Another problem that HVAC maintenance should anticipate is electrical fires.

No matter how efficient they are, all gas-burning furnaces release some carbon monoxide into the air. Not only is carbon monoxide colorless, but it is toxic. Gas can seep into your living area if it isn't appropriately vented out of your roof.

Every year, about 50,000 Americans seek treatment at the emergency department due to carbon monoxide poisoning. And it claims the lives of over 400 individuals. For this reason, whenever we install new HVAC systems, we make sure to include smoke and carbon monoxide monitors.

6. Extended System Life

The longevity of your HVAC system can be greatly extended by getting frequent tune-ups. This implies that you have a long time to put off buying a new HVAC system. Wouldn't it be nice to postpone a significant investment if your system is in fine operating order and should last for another 12 to 20 years?

With preventative maintenance, you shouldn't have to pay any earlier than necessary because a new system might cost thousands of dollars.

Chapter 8

Most Common HVAC Problems

Many of the top 10 HVAC difficulties can be resolved with simple coil and filter cleaning, but if left unattended, many of these issues can grow into much worse problems. Regular preventative maintenance visits can help avert most of these. To avoid disruptions during severe weather, it is advisable to have your system inspected once a year.

GET SOLUTIONS FOR THE TOP 10 COMMON HVAC ISSUE

1) INADEQUATE MAINTENANCE

You MUST schedule routine maintenance by a licensed service contractor to maintain the correct functioning of your system. With routine maintenance performed by a qualified service contractor, many of the most frequent furnace repairs can be avoided. Your home's heating system is probably something you spent hundreds of dollars on. How about safeguarding that investment? If you don't execute routine maintenance, you'll probably face expensive problems, higher energy bills, subpar performance, and dissatisfaction.

Give Jennings Heating a call at (330)574-8503 to arrange for a NATE-certified specialist to inspect your HVAC system and protect your investment and peace of mind.

2) UNCLEAN FILTERS

One of the most crucial things you can do to increase the longevity and effectiveness of your furnace is to replace your filter on a regular basis. Your air conditioner will have to work considerably harder to circulate air around your house if your filter is dirty because it will block ventilation. This will cause comfort problems as well as undue pressure on the fan in your furnace. The furnace may overheat and shut off on high limit due to a filthy filter.

3) IGNITION OR PILOT ISSUES

Numerous factors can lead to ignition issues. A pilot outage, brief cycling, furnace lockout, or delayed burner ignition can all be caused by a filthy pilot, flame sensor, or burners. It can also be the consequence of a malfunctioning gas supply or just the need to repair a worn-out ignition component, such as a thermocouple or hot surface ignitor. In either case, since these issues involve high voltage and natural gas, it is preferable to have a qualified service expert solve them.

4) DEFECTS IN THERMOSTAT USES

Thermostats come in a wide variety, both programmable and non-programmable. The thermostat or the way it is set is often the cause of a homeowner's perceived problems with their furnace. Checking the operating instructions and owner's manual can help you avoid paying for an expensive or pointless service call. Batteries in programmable thermostats may need to be changed on a regular basis. A service technician can rapidly diagnose issues if they are still malfunctioning.

5) TEXTURE AND WEAR MECHANICALLY

Your heating system is dependent on several mechanical parts. The regular wear and tear of these components may have a negative impact on the performance of your equipment. These include bearings and belts, which can lead to problems with ventilation, poor heating, or overheating. Checking for stretched or worn belts and, if needed, oiling bearings and motors should be part of routine maintenance.

6) unusual fan noises

Certain noises produced by the furnace are typical, but others could be an alert or sign of a mechanical issue. An inducer motor or blower motor's failing bearings may be indicated by a whining or screeching motor. It could be necessary to replace the engine in order to prevent a furnace failure. If not, we can install a brand-new furnace from scratch. Dirty burners or problems with ventilation could be the source of other noises. In any case, it's advisable to pay attention to these indicators since they can indicate a hazardous working state or perhaps a furnace failure.

7) BLOWN TRIPPED BREAKERS OR FUSES

Overworking the blower is the most frequent cause of a circuit breaker being tripped by the furnace. Your blower will have to work harder to make up for any obstructions to the airflow in your system. The most frequent reason is an unclean air filter. Your blower will have to work harder to push air through a dirty air filter. This uses more energy from the blower and occasionally trips the circuit breaker. Reset your circuit breaker after checking and replacing your filter with a clean one. It is best to get in touch with a professional if the issue persists so they can safely diagnose whether the problem is related to a furnace malfunction or whether the circuit breaker may have broken. Additional problems that may cause the blower to overwork include unclean coils, closed or blocked air registers, and duct leaks.

8) UNCLEAN EVAPORATOR OR CONDENSER COILS

It's likely that because routine maintenance has been neglected, your air conditioner isn't cooling as well as it could. Your system's coils might become clogged with dirt and debris, which can drastically lower its performance and shorten its lifespan. After turning off the condenser's electricity, you can hose off the outside coil. Electricity can be cut off at the electric panel or at the electrical disconnect close to the condenser. It is possible for the indoor evaporator coil to get dusty, particularly if the furnace filters are not replaced regularly. An unclean evaporator coil might cause your air conditioner and furnace to operate less efficiently and require more effort from you. A qualified service professional will need to clean extremely unclean coils.

9) THE BLOWER NEVER QUITS

A furnace blower may run constantly for several reasons. Inspect the fan switch on the thermostat prior to requesting repair assistance. When the thermostat is in the "fan on" position, the motor will operate nonstop. Homeowners frequently unintentionally turn on the fan by mistake.

The furnace has a fan relay that activates the blower when heat is needed; if the relay sticks, the blower won't switch off. The furnace has a variety of safety features and restrictions. The circuit board has the potential to start the furnace in order to cool it down. The blower won't turn off if the safety or limit doesn't reset. An experienced service technician can assess this issue and provide options for fixing it.

10) LEAKS OF WATER

Condensate is produced by high efficiency furnaces and air conditioners. In order to guarantee appropriate water drainage, drain pipes are used. In the event that the drain lines are fractured or clogged, water may escape from furnaces. Pouring bleach down the drain once in a while will assist a homeowner maintain clean drain lines. The heat exchanger, evaporator drain pan, and collector box are further potential leak sources. It is advisable to get in touch with a service specialist to identify the cause of the water leak and discuss possible fixes.

HVAC Troubleshooting Guide: What to Do Before Calling a Pro

Considering the intricacy of your air conditioning system, using an HVAC troubleshooting guide could be beneficial. It would appear that you would always require a professional when something went wrong with an HVAC system because of the associated price and difficulty of fixing one. On the other hand, there are numerous methods for handling heating, ventilation, and air conditioning problems on your own. Not only are you squandering money on these easy problems, but you're also wasting a technician's time, which they could be using to solve more difficult problems.

Guide to HVAC Troubleshooting

You can save time and money by using these HVAC troubleshooting suggestions before hiring a professional:

1. Examine your air filter.

An unclean or obstructed air filter is among the most frequent causes of air conditioning issues. Look for a dirty filter, and depending on the kind, either clean it or replace it (the thinner the filter, the more frequently it needs to be changed). A blocked filter can strain the system, reduce cooling capacity, and impede airflow. As a result, check the filter once every two months and replace it as needed.

2. Examine your circuit breaker.

It may seem obvious to check if the circuit breaker has tripped or been purposefully turned off when troubleshooting your HVAC system. Simply flip the circuit breaker back on in this situation. Although the panel may be located in a storage closet or hallway in certain homes, it should be in the garage or basement. Verify the AC's functionality after resetting the breaker.

3. Find Out Whether There Has Been a Power Outage

Your HVAC system may stop functioning due to uneven airflow caused by a local power outage. Make sure all of the electrical gadgets in your house, place of business, or workplace are operational and the lights are on. An outage is definitely something to investigate, even though it might not be as evident if you work and/or depend on natural lighting.

4. Check for Blockages in Vents

Air flow may be disrupted if furniture, dust, or other objects are obstructing HVAC vents. Check the grills and vents on your HVAC system, and remove any dust or debris that you notice. Make sure that any adjacent furniture or plants are at least two feet away from any vent openings.

5. Examine the batteries.

Check to see if the thermostat is on. If not, the batteries can be dead, which is something you can easily replace yourself. If the thermostat isn't powered, the system won't function correctly. Until new batteries are fitted, a technician is powerless.

6. Speak with the property's owner or manager.

The first time you ever call an HVAC professional, call the property manager. In the absence of the required authorization, they might not be able to fix your system. Notifying the appropriate parties is also a matter of common politeness.

7. Check the Outside Unit for Debris

Unnoticed, the external unit is frequently disregarded. But branches, leaves, and pretty much anything else can literally choke it out. A suction force draws materials and objects. However, you can rinse them off to clear the debris and get the airflow back. Just make sure the machine is completely off of electricity before you begin to pour water on it.

8. Unfreeze the System

Even in the summer, frost can build up on coils and pipes. Thawing out the unit can be beneficial, even if it takes a few hours. This is especially true if the freezing was caused by misuse (turn it off at the thermostat but leave the fan running). If freezing happens during the next day or two, repeat the procedure. Get in touch with an HVAC specialist if the issue persists for longer than a few days.

Other Crucial Information

It is crucial to understand the operation of your HVAC system and to use it correctly before determining that professional assistance is required.

- Keep your thermostat above 70°F to avoid freezing the system rather than lowering the temperature in your house or place of business.

- The average temperature differential between a property's exterior and inside is 20°F; keep in mind that any air conditioner may find it difficult to offer cooling during hot weather.
- Since sunlight is brightest on the west side of your home, close the blinds and drapes on that side. Reducing the surplus heat will help your air conditioner function properly.

Chapter 9

Your Residential HVAC System; Types, Considerations, and Finding the Right Contractor

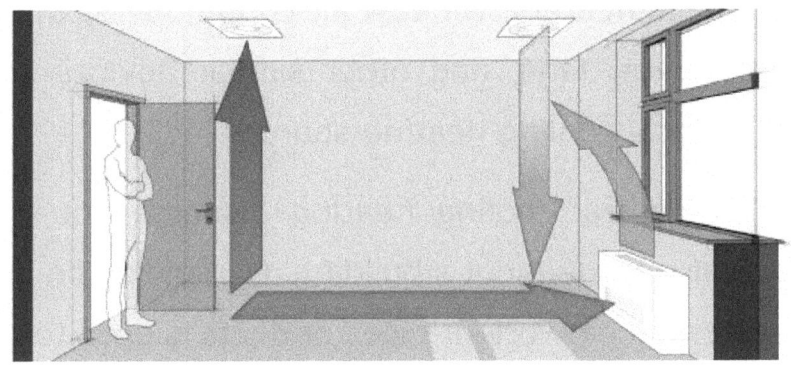

The HVAC system, which stands for heating, ventilation, and air conditioning, is one of the most significant yet troublesome areas of maintenance and repair for many homes. Climate control systems are a crucial component of new construction, home remodeling, and house maintenance that every homeowner will eventually have to deal with.

A fundamental understanding of how each operates is vital because the concepts involved in air conditioner cooling and heating systems differ depending on the type of cooling and heating system employed.

Basics of HVAC Units

There are two types of HVAC systems: central and local. One kind of ductless heating system is local heating, which heats a specific, limited region. Fireplaces, electric radiators, space heaters, window air conditioners, wood and pellet stoves, fans, and other similar devices are examples of local cooling heating sources.

Systems for central cooling heating disperse hot air, steam, or water throughout a building. Depending on the type of system, a network of pipes or ducts is used to do this. For obvious reasons, central heating is the primary source of heat in most places with frigid climates.

A boiler, furnace, or heat pump is a component of a central cooling heating unit. Its purpose is to heat water, steam, or air at a single site before distributing it via ducts or pipes throughout the building.

Pipes receive heated water or steam from a boiler, heat pump, or hydronic heating system. The pipes lead to a radiator, convector, or baseboard heater that provides heat for the entire space. Certain systems just have a single pipe connecting to every fixture, while others have two.

Forced air from a central heating system heats a network of ducts that are positioned in the room's coldest area and link to vents. Usually, this would go along external walls or adjacent to windows to reduce condensation. Cold air is recirculated to the furnace through a second duct system.

Through the flow of indoor and outdoor air, ventilation eliminates heat, smoke, smells, dampness, and airborne microorganisms. making the air better. Naturally, air conditioning also contributes to maintaining a comfortable indoor air quality.

HVAC units perform three interrelated functions: heating, ventilation, and air conditioning. When combined, they offer a pleasant temperature, just the right amount of humidity, and better indoor air quality for comfortable living situations.

Interior Design Tip for Residential HVAC

Organizing an addition to a house or renovating an older house could need expanding the HVAC system. Homeowners ought to be aware of the following:

- The ideal person to help you comprehend the current central system is an experienced special trade contractor, such as a heating and air conditioning contractor or heating ventilating contractor. He or she can decide whether more heating and/or cooling appliances would be sufficient, or if the household HVAC system has to be enlarged to accommodate the new renovation requirements. This could result in significant cost savings on your overall home improvement budget.
- Even seemingly insignificant changes to a space, like adding a bay window or altering the size or form of the room, could call for the installation of more heating ducts. Not just to maintain proper heat, but also to adhere to construction codes.
- Residents of Canada who wish to upgrade or expand their HVAC system but have limited budget may be eligible for government aid. To find out if you qualify for a Canadian government loan, rebate, or grant for home remodeling, visit Can-Grants.com.
- Take this into consideration when planning to finish off your attic or basement to create more

living or workspace. It's not too difficult to expand a forced-air HVAC system in a basement. Adding a few extra ducts is usually all that is needed, and it is something that a capable do-it-yourself homeowner might manage on their own. But it would be even more difficult to run ducts up to the attic.

- It is necessary to add additional pipes and fixtures when expanding a hydronic boiler heating system. Your best bet for a service provider might be a mechanical HVAC contractor or an experienced local plumber.
- Before starting any home improvement job that involves changing the plumbing or wiring or any other aspect of the construction, make sure to check with your local building department. To make sure your project complies with the local building code, make sure you follow the requirements, get any required permissions, and have the work inspected.
- If you have limited budget and your HVAC system cannot accommodate the extra load needed for your home renovation or new room addition, you might want to think about getting additional units.

For example, an electric window air conditioner and baseboard heater. Heaters can be wired to a 240-volt circuit or can plug into a conventional 120-volt outlet; room A/C units typically plug into a 240-volt outlet. This may entail adding a new circuit to your electrical panel, but it will be simpler and less expensive than adding to your home's HVAC system.

Installing a radiant heating system is an additional, and increasingly common, option to growing your cooling heating system. Electrical cables or hot-water tubing hidden below the finished surfaces of walls, ceilings, and floors are used in this method to provide heat.

Large-scale installations of this kind of system require the expertise of a residential general contractor or a specialized profession; this is not a do-it-yourself project.

Employing a Contractor for Your Project to Update or Expand Your HVAC System

The following should be considered while choosing the best contractor for new HVAC installation or HVAC unit expansion:

- Verify a contractor's credentials and licensure before hiring them. To find out if the contractor and/or their business have been the subject of any complaints, contact the Better Business Bureau (BBB).
- Make sure to verify the references you are given. Find out from references whether they were happy with the finished product, whether it was finished on schedule, and if they would hire the contractor again. If not, find out why.
- Choose a contractor with whom you are at ease; someone who takes the time to listen to your inquiries and clarify HVAC jargon, as well as one who completely explains the HVAC needs for your proposed home improvement.
- Ascertain whether the contractor is a member of any regional or national associations or committees. Verify whether they are a current, active member.
- Maintain open channels of communication and be accessible for advice at any time during the project.

- Verify that the quotes you receive from potential contractors are accurate project estimates rather than "eestimates," which are liable to fluctuate.

Selecting HVAC Contractors and the Agreement

Once you've identified two or three contractors you think are qualified candidates, give each one a precise, in-depth project description, then gather quotes. Create a contact with all the information once you've decided which HVAC contractor you feel most comfortable working with.

The legal address of the renovation site as well as the names, addresses, and phone numbers of both parties should be included in the contract. A thorough task description, start and finish dates, a comprehensive materials list, labor and material costs, payment schedules, information on who is in charge of getting permits, and any other relevant information should all be included.

Before you sign the contract, have a meeting with the contractor to go over it. The contract should be signed by the project owner and the contractor, with copies kept for their records.

Additional Things to Think About

You can identify a contractor for your HVAC-related home renovation project through word-of-mouth recommendations. Online resources are growing in popularity and provide a greater range of trustworthy local contractors for selection.

How Does a Commercial HVAC System Work?

Three components are needed to control the climate in a business building: controls, a distribution system, and warm or cool air. The building's cooling air is controlled by the same thermostat and travels via the same ducts as the heated air. But the origin will be different.

Air, warm or cool?

When a commercial HVAC system's heating is turned on, the burners typically produce combustion gas, which is then sent to a heat exchanger to warm the air passing through. Heat pumps can occasionally bring outside heat indoors. Heat pumps and air conditioners function similarly, however air conditioners move heat from inside spaces outside.

Some commercial buildings heat their water using boiler systems; the hot water is sent through pipes that are set into the ceiling, walls, or flooring. Even though the building may not be heating up directly, you will still feel the air getting warmer.

Allocation

Check it out: the idea that warm air rises and cool air falls is helpful when mechanical devices are used to ventilate a structure. Air is constantly being drawn in and taken out, sometimes with heat modifications.

Regulators

Commercial buildings can utilize basic programmable thermostats, similar to those found in homes, to regulate all of this. These thermostats can transmit different heating or cooling queues throughout the day.

More sophisticated direct digital controls (DDC) are also an option for commercial HVAC systems. More sophisticated controls improve the dependability and energy efficiency of commercial structures. Sensors are used by a central computer to automate temperature schedules and lighting controls.

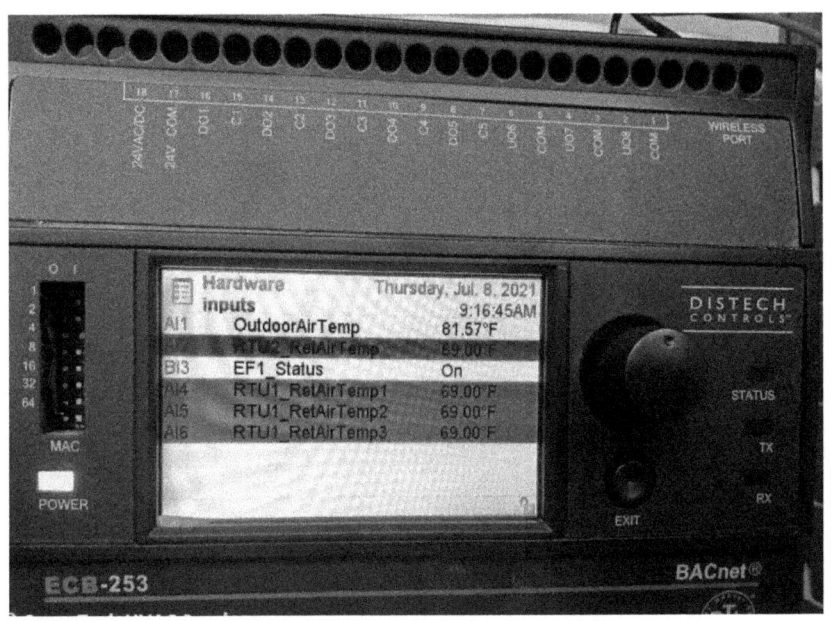

Direct Digital Control Thermostat (DDC) for Commercial HVAC

From a main workstation, staff members can manually respond to and modify settings, enabling users to receive performance updates, resolve issues, and do maintenance. Because of its complexity and adaptability, the DDC is the more costly choice.

Users can apply temperature setbacks to save energy, anywhere from 5% to 20%, using both DDC and basic controls. When the building is empty and the workday is ended, for example, the thermostat is set to a temperature setback, which occurs when no heating or cooling is required.

Just right! You now understand the workings of an HVAC system.

However, there are various kinds.

Types of HVAC Systems for Commercial Buildings

The HVAC system in a business building comes in three primary designs, although there are countless ways to use them.

Systems in packages

Packaged systems are made up of a compressor, condenser, evaporator, and fan coil all in one unit. There is an incorporated thermostat. Buildings without enough space for larger HVAC systems can benefit greatly from packaged units.

In buildings where people must have control over the temperature and air quality in their rooms, such as hotels, hospitals, condominiums, and senior homes, packaged terminal air conditioners are frequently installed in the windows.

Packaged terminal heat pumps work by moving heat from the outside to the interior during the winter and back again during the summer.

Divided systems

Split systems are frequently linked to the ducting of a building, such as in a residential apartment. They are excellent for smaller commercial buildings, such as restaurants, convenience stores, and small offices, since they are perfect for residential buildings. DDC or a thermostat can be used to control each space.

The drawback? You may require a different HVAC unit set for every location you wish to have temperature control over. This clogs the building's exterior or rooftop. It is possible to implement zoning to manage separate spaces, but the cost is high.

One option for simultaneously heating and cooling the various sections of a medium-sized to big commercial building would be to use a variable refrigerant flow system (VRF). VRF systems are uncommon because they are comparatively new in the US. They take warm air from one place to cool it and then transfer it to another that needs heating by using heat pumps or heat recovery systems. Later on, we'll talk more about this technique.

Where is this outdoor unit going, then?

HVAC rooftop RTU

A package unit that is situated on the roof is referred to as a rooftop unit, or RTU. The main parts of the rooftop HVAC units are shielded by weather-resistant housings because they are situated on flat roofs, no higher than ten stories. The compressor, condenser, evaporator, and blower are all housed in one small HVAC unit.

A rooftop unit is a kind of air handler that comes completely completed from the factory; it modifies the air and circulates it through duct systems. A few RTUs are limited to heating, others to cooling, and some to both.

An air hood that allows the RTU to receive air conditioning is located inside its rectangular housing. The air travels via dampers, which are made of revolving metal sheets that control airflow. After passing through the filter, the air is directed onto coils that either heat or cool it. The air is being drawn in by the fan and is then blown into the duct system, which transports it to the intended location.

In order to save energy and maintain safe CO2 levels, an RTU usually uses a combination of indoor and outdoor air on very hot or cold days.

Advantages

- Easy to use and flexible
- Completely integrated HVAC systems
- HVAC that is zoned for optimal performance (each RTU services a single region of the building)
- Reasonable
- Simple to set up
- Silent
- Conserve floor area
- A more secure location
- New, more effective models

Cons:

- Shorter lasting
- Occupy a large amount of area on the roof
- Older models use less energy, which causes power bills to rise.
- Needs greater upkeep

Although RTUs are widely used, your building may also benefit from a less prevalent choice.

Systems VRF

In the US, VRF systems are quite recent. Very complex commercial HVAC systems, VRF systems were developed in Japan in the early 1980s.

VRF systems are ductless, to put it simply. They use heat pumps or heat recovery systems, which transfer refrigerant from a central external unit that houses all the compressors and condensers, in place of ductwork. Each zone's temperature is determined by the rate at which refrigerant is delivered to the interior units. Better temperature customization is made possible by this.

A VRF system's quiet, potent indoor equipment requires very little room. This also means that installation is simple because no ductwork is required and the majority of interior units may fit in a building's elevator.

The efficiency of VRFs surpasses that of ducted HVAC systems by up to 30%. This is because, unlike in conventional systems, less energy is lost through ductwork thanks to the variable compressor speed, which allows for more precise temperature adjustments.

Regretfully, VRF systems are more expensive and need having a backup condenser on standby in case something goes wrong.

What distinguishes this from the HVAC system in your house, then?

How Commercial HVAC Differs From Residential HVAC

Size

Larger buildings require larger HVAC systems to condition and ventilate than residential ones (unless we're talking about Bill Gates' home). You would be right to assume that its components are larger. A commercial system is modular, but its components are grouped together for convenient installation and maintenance, unlike a home system, which consists of a single freestanding unit.

In the US, a typical residential air conditioning unit can weigh up to five tons. The most common sizes for modular rooftop units are 10, 25, and 50 tons. There is an increase in power for the thermostats, condenser fans, compressors, evaporators, blowers, and dampers.

Location

In a residential home, the outdoor unit is typically located outside in the backyard or on the side of the house, and the indoor unit (such as the furnace) is typically located in the basement, closet, or attic. One term for this is a split system. Conversely, HVAC systems in commercial buildings are typically located on the roof, in a utility room in the basement, or elsewhere adjacent to the structure. These are bundled systems, or all-in-one kinds. As previously indicated, the rooftop offers a strong sound barrier, lots of room, and is out of the way.

Conservators

These might be the best-kept secret in business HVAC. By drawing in cool outside air, they use logic controllers and sensors to remove heat from the structure. This is basically free cooling. Reduced energy consumption, reduced HVAC unit wear and tear, and enhanced ventilation all result. The latter is particularly crucial for older structures, as they might not have the benefits of contemporary HVAC systems. Regretfully, home systems do not come with economizers.

Areas

Commercial HVAC systems, in contrast to most domestic HVAC systems, are made up of numerous packaged units, each with its own thermostat, allowing different indoor climates to coexist in a single structure. Because of this, every region is independent of the others and may be fully customized. To minimize interruption, technicians can work on one zone at a time.

Ventilation

Ventilation in commercial buildings is more complicated because of their larger size. Smaller residential structures have more windows per square footage, and opening them is a simple way to relieve stuffy air. Nonetheless, commercial buildings typically require a defined mechanical ventilation system and/or fresh air intake. Additionally, commercial buildings could have labs, restaurants, fitness centers, and other establishments that need a lot of ventilation to maintain a suitable level of indoor air quality.

Drainage

HVAC systems remove moisture from the air while it's heating or cooling. This passes through the piping and overflows into a tray. The primary distinction is that commercial systems will have a larger and more intricate pipe and drain network.

Price

Commercial HVAC systems are influenced by various cost considerations such as building size, installation fees, brand, kind of unit, and company activity. Larger businesses should anticipate to pay between $7.50 and $10.50 per square foot for AC systems, while small firms with one cooling zone can budget between $3 and $4.

Maintenance

Commercial HVAC Upkeep

Commercial systems typically require more expensive repairs. Specialized specialists and a distinct set of tools are required for servicing commercial HVAC equipment. Larger pieces of equipment are frequently situated in hard-to-reach places. Due to the requirement for more regular expert visits, commercial HVAC maintenance is also more expensive. For many firms, in addition to a monthly filter replacement visit, a full scope maintenance visit every quarter is strongly suggested in place of two annual maintenance visits.

We can assist with that, yes.

Nor is that all. Commercial HVAC systems present a distinct set of challenges.

Common Commercial HVAC Problems

Brief Riding

Your compressor will short cycle, as you may hear. Proceed. Cease. Proceed. Cease. a constant restarting of the compressor prior to the cooling cycle ending. Typically, the compressor is operated by the air conditioner or heat pump until the thermostat signals for it to cease. Short cycling can occur for a few different reasons, such as a simple blocked air filter, a malfunctioning thermostat, low refrigerant levels from leaks, etc.

And speaking of that...

Refrigerator Leakage

Leaks in refrigerant are the most frequent problems with commercial air conditioning systems. You might be losing refrigerant if you see oil around your AC's valves, service ports, or connections, or if it's just not blowing cold air. A typical audible queue is short cycling. Refrigerant leaks can damage your HVAC system and cause more serious issues if they are not promptly fixed.

Unclean Filters

We can replace your filters for you. It is recommended that you change your filters four to twelve times a year, or at least once a month. In addition to shielding you from harmful particles, filters preserve the evaporator coil. Since air cannot pass through a clogged filter, air will be drawn through holes, fissures, and other openings by the negative air pressure, dirtying the coil. A dirty coil will have to work twice as hard to heat or cool the air in the building since it cannot perform its job effectively and loses a significant amount of efficiency. Its life is shortened by years of wear and tear.

Filthy Coils in Condensers

This is obvious from a distance of a mile. As you can see, the condenser coils are located outside the building and the evaporator coils are located inside your split-system commercial HVAC unit. Both coils are together in the containment, usually on the roof, of packaged rooftop units. Heat is helped to escape to the outside by the condenser coils. Heat transfer is impeded when they are unclean, which can be caused by a buildup of dust, trash, grass, leaves, animal hair, and other materials. As little as 0.042 inches of dirt on condensing coils might result in a 21% reduction in cooling efficiency, according to an EPA study.

Sounds

There could be a whole symphony of noises coming from your commercial HVAC system. These need to be interpreted as audible cues that something is wrong. The following are examples of possible noises: booming from a pilot light failing to ignite the furnace; squeaking from a lack of lubricant in the motor; vibration from an unbalanced fan; thudding from an encumbered fan; rattling from the blower or loose ducts; buzzing or hissing from a refrigerant leak; and whistling from a boiler due to trapped or blocked air. It's critical to turn off your commercial HVAC system in this situation and contact a specialist straight away.

A malfunctioning energy saver

An economizer aids in lowering cooling energy usage. A damper opens to gather the air for circulation into the commercial HVAC system if the outside air is lower in humidity and colder than the interior air. The economizer's air temperature sensors may malfunction or the dampers may become stuck if it isn't working at a specific outside temperature. To what extent is this an issue? In a study by the New Building Institute, economizers were broken in over two thirds of the 500 RTUs that were looked at.

obstructed drain

Moisture is gathered on the coil and condenses as the refrigerant in the evaporator coils changes from a liquid to a gas. After that, the water is meant to go down a drain. If the drain isn't properly maintained, slime accumulation could obstruct it. If this occurs, the water will corrode or damage the building, your air quality will decrease, and you will smell stale or moldy air coming from the vents.

Evaporator Belt Looseness

A loose belt slows down the fan's speed, strains the pulley, and finally causes the coil to freeze. Your evaporator belt won't last as long if it's loose. A loose belt on your business air conditioner may be indicated by noise or a decrease in airflow.

Better yet, give us a call.

So, how do you stay clear of all these issues?

Commercial Air Conditioning Upkeep

Regular maintenance for your car or kitchen appliances is just as critical as that of your commercial HVAC system. A simple investment in prevention can also save you a lot of money, just like any other upkeep.

The fundamental advantage of maintaining commercial HVAC systems is that each component's lifespan is extended. One horrible performer degrades the entire play because of how their roles overlap. The primary problem with broken or clogged HVAC components is that they increase the strain on the heating and cooling system's ability to function. When combined with typical wear and tear, this significantly shortens the lifespan of your commercial air conditioning system by eight to fifteen years.

It's critical to have constant indoor air quality. Have you ever noticed that your breathing changed when you entered an older building? or do your eyes well up? Unwanted particles have most likely entered the air, and the filthy coils, filters, or blower parts may have been easily discovered with a quick maintenance check. Poor indoor air quality is particularly detrimental to retail establishments, as their success depends on customers having a favorable in-store experience.

Cutting expenses is essential to operating a business. You would not want to add expensive energy bills to your never-ending list of expenditures. Energy expenses for commercial HVAC systems can be reduced by 5 to 40% with preventative maintenance. Poor maintenance results in weakened parts, which not only reduces the equipment's lifespan but also makes it work harder to achieve its goals.

You need a detailed, personalized plan to keep your HVAC system maintained. In order to adequately heat, cool, and ventilate the air in large commercial buildings, an enormously intricate network of HVAC equipment is needed. This implies that a prefabricated HVAC maintenance program is not reliable. It's critical to get assistance from an HVAC service company. To create a checklist, they will take into account factors like the equipment kind, budget, and climate.

You'll differ in how frequently you complete maintenance activities. You can be more forgiving in temperate regions, and you might need to check on them every month in harsher ones. In any case, four yearly services ought to be included in every commercial maintenance program.

Owners, managers, and superintendents of business buildings often have the poor habit of putting off maintenance for their commercial HVAC systems until something goes wrong. Refrain from joining them. To prevent circumstances where you have to spend and lose a lot of money to stop operations and start HVAC repairs, make sure you and your staff have a checklist similar to the one below.

Typically, an HVAC check list will consist of:

- Keeping an eye out for general sounds or odors
- Changing the air filters
- Examining the operation and settings of the thermostat
- Cleaning up dirt, dust, and debris, paying particular attention to registers and air intakes
- Examining cables and other electrical parts
- Cleaning the drains and pans
- Inspecting pipes for leaks or corrosion
- Examining seals
- Examining insulation and air ducts
- Examining previous year's costs for cooling and heating

- Examining and sanitizing every part, both internal and external
- Arranging for expert maintenance

Keep in mind that every building is unique and needs a separate checklist. Upgrades can be made for increased efficiency if needed.

Chapter 10

Advancements in HVAC System Technology

The hardware and software landscape is expanding quickly, leading to fast changes in HVAC system technology. Look for these technologies to help modernize and improve your home's performance if you wish to increase its efficiency.

Energy-Use Analysis Software

The use of various softwares may be the most important innovation and technology impacting HVAC systems, despite the fact that there are many others. New methods of controlling and utilizing HVAC systems will be made possible by applications that are connected to the air conditioner, furnace, and vents.

A large portion of this program will be used for energy use analysis. These softwares will enable technicians, engineers, architects, and builders to design systems that have real-time energy analysis capabilities. HVAC professionals' choices, designs, and implementations of heating and cooling systems will also be influenced by new advancements.

Controlled Temperature via Motion Sensor

The HVAC system in the majority of American homes must be set to a precise temperature; adjusting the thermostat directly was the only option to modify the airflow or the temperature. However, designers can create networks that literally change the settings when a move is detected by syncing motion sensors with the HVAC system.

This is how it could operate: the HVAC system will be turned off or on low if the room is empty. The device has the ability to raise the temperature to enhance comfort as soon as it senses movement in the space.

Many Heat Sources in a Single System

At the moment, almost all heating systems rely on a single heat source. Electric or natural gas furnaces will be required if you need one. Each have particular benefits and downsides, and one might be better suited for a given home. Still, it seems absurd to restrict a heating system to a single source when there are so many alternatives.

Modern HVAC technology enables the use of different heat sources. It's possible that heating systems combine several heating sources; in order to produce the most effective heating, a heat pump and furnace will cooperate.

For instance, some energy sources function best at extremely cold temperatures, thus if the outside temperature is approximately 40 degrees, the system may use electricity; if the temperature approaches 30 degrees, the system may switch to an alternative energy source.

Complete Home Fans

Whole house fans have been in use for a number of decades. These days, they can reduce cooling expenditures by up to 90% in regions like California because to advancements in energy efficiency.

The way a whole house fan HVAC system operates is by forcing hotter interior air into the attic and drawing in cooler outdoor air through open windows. Whole house fans are a ventilation system, as opposed to an air conditioner, which cools the air inside a house.

Ice-Used Air Conditioners

There were refrigerators in the 1930s that drew their chilly air directly from ice. Though it may sound archaic, contemporary designers are discovering that using ice to cool a home's air can really save electricity.

Presently in development are new systems that produce ice overnight, store it, and use it to cool a building all day. This type of technology is thought to be able to significantly minimize a building's energy usage, which would lower energy costs and lessen the building's carbon impact for homes or businesses.

HVAC Enclosure

The idea of zoning may be the subject of greater discussion in the HVAC industry than any other technology currently under development. The way this system operates is by dividing the house into different sectors and distributing warm or cold air to each one as needed.

You can lower the temperature on the first level and maintain a higher one upstairs, saving energy instead of heating the entire house. Alternatively, you may lessen airflow to a room that isn't being used, like a guest bedroom, based on how the house has been zoned. It is anticipated that zoning will increase energy efficiency in residences and office buildings by permitting the strategic use of airflow.

Pumps for Geothermal Heat

Even though this technology is not particularly new, it is becoming more and more used in a variety of contexts. People have realized in recent years how effective this technology can be as a source of electricity for their homes, which can power a variety of equipment including air conditioning and heating. You might even use it to warm water.

In addition to taking heat from the earth and using it to heat a house, geothermal heat pumps may also be used in the other direction, sending heat into the ground and away from the house when you need cool air. In order to help warm water, geothermal energy can also be employed, which eliminates the need for gas or electricity.

Underfloor Radiant Heating

Many homeowners are actually adopting this technology, and it might be accessible for your house right now. With this technique, heating units are essentially installed in the floor, warming the surface and producing heat that radiates upward, warming the whole house. While electrical systems can also be a part of radiant flooring, warm water circulation pipes provide the majority of the heat. This is a fantastic way to improve the comfort level in your house and a very effective source of home warmth.

Sensor-Induced Airflow

It seems that one of the key instruments propelling the technological development of HVAC systems would be sensors. Not only may sensors be used to control temperature and air power, but they can also be utilized to control vents. The homes of the future with HVAC systems will probably have sensors in every room. These sensors have the ability to measure motion and room temperature. Using this data, the vents in a room can be automatically adjusted. The vents can automatically change if the sensors determine that warm or cool air is not required in that particular room.

Air Conditioners Printed in 3D

During the past ten years, 3D printing has developed quickly, enabling the creation of smaller, more detailed goods and parts. Air conditioning systems can now be 3D printed because technology has advanced to the point where smaller parts needed for these kinds of appliances can now be produced. Bricks that are 3D printed and have the ability to extract moisture from the air mean that the technology can even be used as a dehumidifier.

While 3D printing might not be practical for extremely hot or cold climates just yet, it could lower the price of these devices and improve the comfort of houses without air conditioning.

Using Computer Heat to Warm a House or Structure

Overheating is an ongoing battle for your computer. The computer will automatically turn on a fan to cool its internal components if it senses that it is working too hard and getting too warm. What if, however, it were possible to capture all that heat and utilize it to warm a house or other structure? That's just what some developers are envisioning, and they believe it may be the next big thing in energy-efficient green buildings.

Reducing the total cost of heating during a winter month may be possible by utilizing the available heat. This technique appears to be particularly helpful in commercial and office environments when numerous computers are in use simultaneously. Even if one computer might not be sufficient, dozens or even hundreds of them could generate enough heat to warm a building, or at least enough to cut down on the amount of gas or electricity needed.

Incredible Air Purifiers from a Reputable Brand

Additionally, residential air quality improvement technologies are developing quickly. After a lot of development, air purifiers are currently among the most crucial household products.

Your house or business will always have clean, fresh air if you use an air purifier or one with activated carbon and other technologies.

Sustainable HVAC systems in commercial construction: balancing comfort and energy efficiency

Systems for air conditioning, ventilation, and heating are necessary for any kind of business. Although they aid in preserving suitable indoor temperatures and humidity levels, their high energy usage may raise questions.

We will examine the many approaches to developing sustainable HVAC systems and how they can contribute to lowering emissions while maintaining a high level of comfort.

Appropriate air balance

One of the easiest ways to improve energy efficiency is to balance your HVAC system. This procedure lowers waste and guarantees that your HVAC system operates at peak efficiency. Controlling airflow inside the system, performing leakage tests, and modifying pressure levels are all part of balancing. These actions can improve HVAC system efficiency and result in long-term energy cost savings.

Additionally, this procedure is necessary to keep the quality of the air indoors high. It contributes to ensuring that the air in our houses and workplaces is pure and free of pollutants. The amount of airborne irritants that cause respiratory issues can be decreased with proper ventilation.

Maintaining it at its best requires routine maintenance. Installing access door HVAC can help this process along and make maintenance tasks more accessible and effective. In addition to reducing downtime and maintaining system efficiency, these doors can increase the system's lifespan and ultimately result in cost savings.

Making use of heat pumps

As we work to build sustainable and energy-efficient houses, heat pumps play a bigger role. With the use of refrigerants, heat pumps provide an economical and effective means of heating and cooling buildings by transferring heat energy from the surrounding air or ground to the regions that require it.

Although these systems perform best in temperate regions, they might be ineffective in extremely hot or cold weather. The US Department of Energy believes that heat pumps have a bright future despite their current difficulties. Since heat pumps are entirely electric, using renewable energy to power them prevents greenhouse gas emissions. Compared to conventional gas-powered heating systems that produce pollutants, this quality is noticeably superior.

The Residential Cold Climate Heat Pump Challenge is a program launched by the Department of Energy with the goal of increasing heat pump efficiency. It requires producers to create cold climate heat pumps (CCHPs) that are dependable and efficient, specifically designed for two different temperature ranges: -15°F (-26°C) and 5°F (-15°C).

As of right now, the project is in the field testing phase. By 2024, a lot more manufacturers should be releasing their cold-climate heat pumps.

Including solar energy systems

When it comes to renewable energy, integrated photovoltaic systems are revolutionizing the industry. This new method enables the installation of solar cells without the need for extra components by integrating glass and roofing materials. This feature saves time and money by streamlining the installation process. Businesses may benefit from solar energy and effectively and economically lessen their carbon impact with this integrated solution.

In order to guarantee optimal performance, cooling solar cells is crucial when integrating a photovoltaic system into a building. Solar cells can be cooled by using the building's natural convection or its conditioned relief to lower their temperature, which increases the cells' output and efficiency. In hot climates where solar cell temperatures can rise dangerously high, cooling is important.

Making use of a trombe wall

The Trombe wall is a cutting-edge passive method that uses solar radiation to heat an area. How it operates is that the heat from the sun is captured by a building called a "greenhouse," from which it is then released into the space.

The air's heat is trapped between a glass and a wall during the day. If the heat source is behind a 38 cm or thicker wall, it takes 8–10 hours for the heat to spread to other areas of the building. This arrangement emits heat all night long and maintains a comfortable temperature during the day.

Controlling the amount of heat gained and lost at night can offer a practical and affordable means of keeping a space warm during the chilly winter months. This technique not only reduces energy expenses but also benefits the environment because it runs without the need for fuel or additional electricity.

Choosing the appropriate environmentally friendly parts for your sustainable HVAC system

Because of the growing worry over climate change, your enterprises are going to require more and more energy-efficient components. It is beneficial to take the necessary steps to establish a sustainable HVAC system.

The type of device you need, its energy efficiency rating, and any additional features that might improve its performance should all be carefully considered when selecting the most sustainable and energy-efficient cooling/heating systems for your company.

Benefits Of Transforming Your Properties Into Smart Buildings

A smart building is a structure that makes use of cutting-edge technology through the installation of AI, IoT devices, linked sensors, or building management systems that gather and transmit data to enable real-time building system monitoring and control.

Both the building's inhabitants and the property owner can benefit greatly from turning homes into smart buildings.

Let's examine the nine advantages of turning your building into a smart building in more detail.

Superb Knowledge and Up-to-Date Information

The capacity to gather and evaluate real-time data is one of the biggest advantages of turning your building into a smart building. IoT devices and connected sensors, such as LoRaWAN technology, may monitor temperature, humidity, occupancy, and energy usage, among other things. Building managers can enhance building performance and boost energy efficiency by using this data to inform their decisions.

For instance, building managers can spot areas of energy waste and take action to address them by keeping an eye on trends of energy consumption. This can entail installing energy-efficient lighting fixtures, modifying HVAC settings, or replacing equipment.

It is also possible to improve occupant comfort and wellbeing by utilizing real-time data. For example, sensors can sense whether a space is too hot or too cold and then change the temperature on their own to provide the best possible comfort.

Lower Energy Bills and Consumption

Making your building a smart building can dramatically cut energy usage and energy costs by optimizing building efficiency based on real-time data insights.

Energy-efficient heating, cooling, and lighting systems that are tuned based on occupancy patterns and real-time data are used in smart buildings to achieve this. For instance, energy-saving adjustments to the HVAC and lighting systems can be made automatically when a room is unoccupied.

Building managers can also save energy costs by reducing consumption by identifying places where energy waste is taking place. Because carbon emissions are decreased, this helps the environment in addition to the bottom line.

Lower Operating Expenses

Smart buildings can drastically lower operating costs in addition to energy expenditures. Smart buildings can minimize maintenance requirements and the need for manual interventions by optimizing building performance through the use of real-time data. As a result, there are fewer incidences of downtime and reduced labor expenditures.

Automated building management systems can also decrease the requirement for manual intervention by streamlining activities. For example, building managers can monitor and control building systems remotely from a central dashboard, which eliminates the need for manual adjustments and on-site visits.

Predictive Upkeep and Reduced Hazards

Predictive maintenance techniques that greatly minimize downtime and diminish the chance of equipment failure are also made possible by smart building technologies. Building managers can spot any problems before they get serious and take preventative action by using real-time data to monitor equipment performance.

Additionally, emergency repairs, which can be expensive and inconvenient for building residents, are less common when predictive maintenance is implemented. Building managers can limit downtime and guarantee optimal building system performance by taking early measures to fix equipment faults.

Building Management Automation

The capacity to automate building management is a key advantage of smart buildings. Building management systems (BMS) give you the ability to remotely operate lighting, security, HVAC (heating, ventilation, and air conditioning), and other systems. From a single interface, you can modify settings, create schedules, set alarms, and track performance. This degree of control gives tenants a more convenient and comfortable living environment in addition to increasing the effectiveness of building management.

Enhancing the Comfort and Well-Being of Occupants

There are various ways that smart buildings might improve tenant comfort and well-being. IoT sensors can keep an eye on temperature, humidity, and air quality within buildings to provide the best possible circumstances for productivity and wellness. Additionally, based on occupancy, BMS systems can modify HVAC and lighting settings to save energy and maintain a comfortable environment. In order to increase safety and hygiene, smart buildings can also offer technologies like voice-activated controls, contactless payment, and touchless entrance.

Increasing Productivity and Work Efficiency

Smart buildings have the potential to greatly increase production and work efficiency. Building managers can monitor and control the building environment in real-time with IoT sensors and BMS systems, making quick adjustments to optimize indoor conditions and energy use. In order to maximize space utilization and guarantee that workplaces are used effectively and efficiently, smart buildings can also make use of occupancy data. Furthermore, smart buildings can offer amenities like automatic maintenance scheduling, scheduling of meeting spaces and resources, and remote access to building systems, all of which can raise building occupant productivity.

Increasing the Building's Security

There are various ways that smart buildings might improve building security. Access control systems, motion detectors, and cameras are examples of Internet of Things devices that can monitor and manage building access while identifying and addressing possible threats. Additionally, BMS systems have the ability to recognize and notify building management of any unexpected activity, including changes in humidity, temperature, or air quality that may pose a security risk. Additionally, automated reactions to security risks, such closing doors or setting off alarms, can be provided by smart buildings.

Increasing Your Assets' Value

For all the reasons listed above, owning a smart building can dramatically raise the value of your property. In fact, smart buildings use less energy and have reduced running expenses, which increases their affordability and appeal to potential buyers. Additionally, improved comfort, convenience, and security are provided by smart buildings, which may make them more appealing to tenants and other building occupants. Buildings with high levels of comfort and security, sustainability, and energy efficiency can command a premium price from investors and buyers of real estate.

Conclusion

To sum up, there are many real advantages to turning your buildings into smart buildings. Smart buildings are superior to traditional buildings in many ways, from lower energy usage and operating costs to enhanced tenant comfort and well-being. Smart buildings can improve your facility's performance and appeal to renters and occupants by automating building management, enhancing security, and raising the value of your assets.

In the future, we should anticipate seeing an increasing number of properties converted into smart buildings as technology develops. Those who invest in smart building technology, such as property owners and managers, will be in a strong position to reap these advantages and maintain their competitive edge in the real estate market.